DATE DUE

MR 25 '97			
JY 11 97			
JE 18 '99			
DE 15 00			
AP 21 04			
MY 15 06			
JE 0 7 '08			

DEMCO 38-296

White House to Your House

White House to Your House: Media and Politics in Virtual America

Edwin Diamond and Robert A. Silverman

The MIT Press
Cambridge, Massachusetts
London, England

Second printing, 1996

© 1995 Massachusetts Institute of Technology

This book was set in Bembo by Wellington Graphics and was printed and bound in the United States of America.

Library of Congress Cataloging-in-Publication Data

Diamond, Edwin.
  White House to your house : media and politics in virtual America
  / Edwin Diamond and Robert A. Silverman.
    p.   cm.
  Includes bibliographical references and index.
  ISBN 0-262-04150-2 (hc : alk. paper)
  1. Presidents—United States—Election. 2. Communication in politics—United States. 3. Communication—Political aspects—United States. 4. Mass media—Political aspects—United States.
  I. Silverman, Robert A., 1971–   . II. Title.
JK528.D53   1995
324.7′3′0973—dc20   95-22501
                                                                          CIP

Contents

Preface

At one daft point in the mid-1990s, the authors of the number-one and number-two best-selling books in America were talk-show divas Rush Limbaugh and Howard Stern. The president of the United States marked an anniversary of his time in office by taking calls from listeners on CNN's *Larry King Live,* the same show on which H. Ross Perot announced his candidacy for president in 1992. And, in a climax of sorts, Newt Gingrich, the congressman from Cobb County, Georgia, as well as the didactic host of a satellite-TV college course, became the new Speaker of the House of Representatives, and through his use of photo opportunities, arguably the most powerful politician in America. Some call this democracy, the triumph of "plain-talking"—in Stern's case, dirty-talking—populism. Conservative comic, genital humorist, campaigner president, billionaire salesman, suburban Savonarola: these five men could not be more different. Yet they share a common ability to use the new-media formats that have become the electronic hearth around which millions of Americans now gather. Our political leaders have learned how to entertain (some of) us, and our entertainers know how to politicize (some others of) us.

Now the 1996 campaign is under way, and there is a new gathering place: the linked computers of the Internet and the commercial online services, home to an estimated 30 million users (more if the new Microsoft Network attracts, and holds, fresh converts). The initiated can log onto the NewtWatch site on the World Wide Web and read details of every aspect of the public life of Newt Gingrich: how much he earns, the full text of the three complaints filed against him in the spring of 1995 by the House Ethics Committee. More neutral data, including voting records going back to 1981, also are available at the site, which can be reached by navigating to http://www.cais.com/newtwatch. A Democratic Party loyalist sponsors the Newt site, but the online world also has empowered ordinary citizens. A year before the 1996 New Hampshire primary, a citizen activist posted a note to the Eastern section of the CompuServe Information Service Republican Forum, asking users to advise her on a guest list for a proposed Tupperware-style party at her home for Lamar Alexander, one of the early announced candidates. At Delphi's PolitiNet, in that same pre-primary period, a user from California posted a message warning New Hampshire voters about his state's governor, Pete Wilson. In 1992, C-SPAN turned its cameras on New Hampshire town meetings, bringing local-citizen voices to a national audience; in 1996, online media will bring national-citizen voices to local races. The hypermedia of chat rooms and bulletin boards is taking its place alongside the traditional media; Dan Rather and Tom Brokaw now vie with every online Tom and Dan for attention.

The shift from the old one-to-many communications model stirs talk of a brave new world of many-to-many communications. Politics, the enthusiasts say, can be made democratic, participatory, open, exuberant—in a word, enjoyable.

The triumph of politics-as-entertainment and entertainment-as-politics speeds the transformation of the national landscape. In the pages that follow we trace the emergence of a place that looks like a real democracy, and a real country, but is in fact a construct, like reality but not real. It is Virtual America.

Introduction: Pop Goes Politics

The president can "get isolated behind the walls of the White House," Bill Clinton was explaining. "We've got to find a way to cut through the isolation." Ted Koppel nodded. The ABC newsman understood. Indeed, Koppel and his *Nightline* staff were prepared to help the president connect with the citizenry—if he did so on ABC. Clinton had allowed Koppel and his camera crew to travel alongside the candidate during the last three days of the 1992 presidential campaign. The result, a stunning bit of cinema verité called "72 Hours to Victory: Behind the Scenes with Bill Clinton," was broadcast on ABC in prime time on the first Thursday after the Tuesday election. Koppel and his producers were so pleased with their television coup that they began thinking of sequels to propose to the new president—"A Day in the Life of the Clinton Transition" . . . "A Day in the Life of Bill and Hillary in the White House" . . . "They'll do what they think will help them," Koppel, the realist, told us. "Remember, almost 60 percent of the electorate voted against him."

All media transactions involve some sort of trade-off between newsmaker and news reporter. Clinton invited ABC News aboard his campaign plane in order to get a specific message across; in the case of "72 Hours to Victory," the image sought was that of the indefatigable but serene campaigner, recorded with an eye on posterity (and the six out of ten doubters). ABC went along for the ride to get one hour of compelling product, a competitive edge unavailable on any other channel. Each side, White House and press corps, uses, or tries to use, the other side. So what else is new? In the 1990s, however, the access adagio came with some fresh steps. The Clinton campaign was imaginatively choreographed, a performance suited to the stage of contemporary media; the White House years were less sure-footed. Most important of all, however, the stage itself changed, stirring fears as old as the Republic and as current as A.M. talk radio.

Our overall purpose is to analyze the performers and their stage in national campaigns as well as in the period between presidential elections, formally known as governance, but now also recognized as the permanent campaign. Accounts of the 1992 presidential election described it in generational, ideological, and economic terms: for example, the displacement of the World War II generation (Ronald Reagan, George Bush, James Baker) by a younger breed of leaders, or the triumph of activist politics over laissez-faire market forces. These factors obviously played a part in the campaign. Less clear, however, is the role of media and communications and the ways that the technologies of the wired nation were reshaping American public life.

In the 1990s, public officials and citizens, leaders and led, hosts and listeners, were instantly in touch with each other. The world was opening up on people's desktops, as home computers, television sets, and telephones rapidly converged into a single powerful multimedia tool. The audience no longer was passive; it began to interact, shaping the entertainment, educational, informational, and political materials that in the past flowed exclusively from producer to consumer. Talk radio, twenty-four-hour television, tabloid news, 1-800 numbers, and online computer services kept us all connected, as the AT & T advertisement reminded viewers. Sometimes that connection was exhilarating: a revealing moment in one of the candidates' televised debates, a memorable phrase at a town meeting. Too often, though, the connections turned ugly, polarized, bitter. Character assassination became routine on talk shows; hate messages were posted on computer bulletin boards, electronic rumormongering bounced through the ether, from office fax to drive-time radio to the late-night news wrap-up; flat-out lies were delivered casually between commercial breaks. Modern technology has resuscitated a kind of Know-Nothing populism, shooting a jolt of electricity through the corpse. The creature now walks, and talks endlessly.[1]

Worse, it sometimes dons the camouflage uniform of far-right private militias, who echo the riffs of the talk culture. Inevitably, the superheated rhetoric led to chillingly maniacal deeds. When a bomb explosion devastated a federal office building in Oklahoma City in the spring of 1995, killing 168 people, the president of the United States speculated that the constant yammer of the talk-show culture itself may have contributed to the paranoid fantasies of the perpetrators.

In memory, the 1992 presidential race has a kind of antique charm: the first talk-show campaign. As Clinton hinted to Koppel, the new administration planned on using the same technologies to reach out from his bully pulpit—selectively, of course, the way *Nightline* was tapped—and produce a talk-show government. The performance began, and the White House walls tumbled, but not in the way the president and his staff had envisioned.

"Larry King Liberated Me"

1

Presidential campaigns have been moving indoors from stump speeches and ballpark rallies to living room TV sets during the past fifty years. In 1992, the primaries and general election took place mainly on soft-media formats, such as the call-in shows, the morning interview programs, and the candidates' joint prime-time appearances. The latter were more like the *Donahue* show than Oxford Rules debates. They were performances, and therein lay much of their popular appeal.

The hard-news TV shows, the prestige newspapers, and the news weeklies—the mainstream press made up of ABC, NBC, CBS, the *New York Times,* the *Washington Post,* the *Los Angeles Times, Time, Newsweek* et al.—became consumers of the "products" created by the soft shows, along with the rest of us. When Ross Perot went on the new-media *Larry King Live* show to announce that he would become a candidate for president of the United States if "the people" wanted him, the old-line network news shows picked up and amplified the video materials from King's easy-listening format. In the candidates' second televised debate in Richmond, Virginia, on the evening of October 15, 1992, Clinton appeared to handle a question from a young woman in the auditorium better than Bush; that is, when Clinton projected a telegenic empathy and a mastery of video skills, the home audience responded favorably. Clinton's ratings shot up in the moments following the debate (according to the telephone polls conducted on behalf of news organizations). The next morning and over the next several days, the major newspapers and commentators awarded victory in the debate to Clinton. The news mainstream followed, where once it had led. In each case, the citizens who gave a "mandate" to Perot or declared Clinton's "victory" were the viewers gathered in front of their television sets.

The Perot candidacy, in fact, existed mainly on soft-format television; he did little traditional campaigning, keeping news conferences and stump speeches to an absolute minimum. But then Clinton also used soft formats, for example, appearing on a ninety-minute talk show with young voters on MTV, the music video channel. Viewers saw Clinton respond to questions put by hostess-anchor Tabitha Soren, twenty-four, and other twentysomethings in a studio audience assembled in Los Angeles. Soren's queries and those of the audience were thoughtful and well phrased. She *sounded* like a network newswoman, further blurring distinctions between hard news and entertainment formats and between citizen questioners and the journalist "professionals." This was just the beginning of the user-friendly revolution. Clinton, Perot, and, belatedly, George Bush, and their running mates, made thirty-nine separate appearances on *Larry King Live, CBS This Morning, Good Morning America, Today,* and the syndicated talk shows from September 1 to October 19. In 1984, and again in 1988, Phil Donahue tried to persuade various presidential candidates to appear on his program; they turned him down—it was not dignified enough. In the spring of 1992, by contrast, both Clinton and Jerry Brown, the former governor of California, sought out Donahue; he ended up inviting them to appear together on his show.

By the fall, even the traditionalist Bush had changed strategy, making a surprise appearance on NBC's *Today* show, when anchor Katie Couric was at the White House interviewing Mrs. Bush. Before that walk-on, Bush had expressed distaste at the idea of the president of the United States appearing on "some weird talk show." In the last week of the race, the increasingly desperate Bush finally granted MTV reporter Soren an interview; he looked about as comfortable with Soren as a father talking to his teenage daughter about safe sex. But perhaps the most startling iconography of the soft revolution was created when Clinton, wearing shades and carrying a saxophone, appeared on the late-night entertainment show featuring the African-American host, Arsenio Hall. While the appearance seemed like one more staged photo-op, it was actually information rich, making generational and racial points simultaneously. It also showed Clinton's clever reading of the subtexts of late-night television: his campaign was demographically sophisticated enough to realize that, for the purposes of its candidate, the middle-brow Jay Leno program would be too square and the ironist David Letterman's program too hip.

The 1992 campaign did not just go populist in its search for the audience-voter; it also consciously sought out interactive formats. The voters' participation, as well as their dollars, were actively solicited. Jerry Brown worked the soft media while plugging his 1-800 fundraising number at every opportunity; for those who missed his TV appearances, there were the Brown bumper stickers—"Dare to Care: Brown 1-800-426-1112." Brown folded his show, but not before some 280,000 callers had pledged $6.5 million to his campaign. The call-in and pledge scheme had been lifted from the script of televangelists like the Reverend Jerry Falwell, who used the television pulpit to gather the faithful in the 1970s and 1980s. As if to affirm that Gutenberg still lived in the age of Larry King, Paul Tsongas passed out more than 140,000 copies of his eighty-five-page book, *A Call to Economic Arms*. Improbably, the underfinanced Tsongas managed to stay afloat—until the Clinton campaign appropriated both Brown's 1-800-number idea and Tsongas's offer of literature.

The Clinton people set up their toll-free number to do more than simply extend an electronic collection plate; it was also designed to assuage callers' doubts about the "character issue." Neatly combining soft formats and interactive politics, Clinton used a sixty-second TV spot to advertise his fifteen-page "Clinton Plan." In addition, the Clinton staff mailed the booklet to every registered voter in New Hampshire. With their candidate's likely voter percentage stuck in the low thirties, the Bush campaign belatedly and tentatively made some interactive efforts; the Republican reelection committee, for example, began using a teleconferencing program to link party officials and workers.

The answer to how effective these techniques were depends on who is asked. The Clinton campaign credited the candidate's interactive television appearances with stopping his plunge in the New Hampshire polls in the days after Gennifer Flowers materialized with her tapes and lurid stories of a long-running affair with then-Governor Clinton. Candidate Clinton was on television five nights in a row in New Hampshire the week before the Tuesday primary. On Thursday, for example, the Clinton campaign bought thirty minutes of time on New Hampshire's biggest commercial station so its candidate could hold a "town-hall meeting" with undecided voters. The next night, Clinton took unscreened telephone calls for thirty minutes, also on commercial television. Throughout the campaign year, too, Clinton and Perot consistently tried to go "over the heads of the professionals"—the journalists from the mainstream media—to reach "the real people," as the formulaic patter put it.

In past years, the rhetorical modes of presidential campaigning had been defined by the candidates' thirty-second spots, by the point-counterpoint structure of formal news conferences, as well as by the framing techniques of newspaper news stories and the old-line networks' nightly television broadcasts. Control of the message was not strictly in the hands of the candidates: they had to share power with professional journalists. In 1992, the press-candidate balance shifted favorably, from the candidates' point of view. The new pop-media forms and the interactive techniques were intended to allow the politicians' *unfiltered* messages to enter the hearts and minds of the American voters. "You know why I can stiff you on the press conferences?" Bill Clinton half-joked in remarks at the Radio and Television Correspondents Association dinner in March 1993, at the beginning of his second year in the White House. "Because Larry King has liberated me from you by giving me to the American people directly."

Partisans of this "liberation" pictured the public as an active participant in the electoral process. Not only was the audience/citizen receiving information, but individuals were able to respond (in some cases, immediately), contributing their own concerns to the electronic dialogue and bringing politics back to the people. Or so went the optimists' spin on the new media environment.

Political participation *was* up somewhat in 1992; more people voted as a percentage of those registered than in any presidential election since 1960. For one, an aging population meant that proportionately more Americans were eligible to vote. For another, economic concerns—worries about jobs, the federal deficit, America's perceived declining role, etc.—brought more voters to the polls. The pop campaign, with its interactive attractions, probably contributed to the higher turnout as well; by some estimates the new formats may have attracted as many as 1 million voters[1] Pop and interactive formats appear to represent the next development in politics, and in the audience's tastes. If they are the wave of the future, however, not everyone looks forward to being carried away.

Once upon a time long ago, before television, the leaders of the two political parties met in private and decided whom to put on the ticket; they ran the campaigns and made sure the faithful marched to the polls on election day. Then came television, and by the beginning in the 1960s, a new kind of politics. The power to tap this man as front-runner or that man as presidential timber deserving of the viewers' attention passed from the parties to Walter Cronkite and his counterparts at the other two major networks, to the columnists and commentators of the *New York Times,* the *Washington Post,* the weekly magazines, and a few other representatives of Big Print. "The screening committee," David Broder, the *Washington Post* columnist, once called these new power brokers (Broder himself holds a lifetime chair on the committee).

In 1992, while nobody but the audience was paying attention, the center of political power shifted again. When Bill Clinton and Jerry Brown faced each other head to head on *Donahue* after the briefest of introductions by the host, viewers watched one hour of pure talking heads. The Clinton-Brown dialogue ended, practically speaking, with both men having almost nothing left to say; they had covered "the issues" in a way that candidates are always urged to do. The *New York Times,* no fan of Donahue or the rest of the pop-media culture, was nearly speechless, too, arguing that voters got a truer picture of Clinton and Brown from Donahue than "from all the rest of television coverage combined." Similarly, Jerry Brown's repeated incantations of his 1-800 mantra produced snickers among the professionals; nevertheless, he demonstrated that a candidate could raise campaign money, create news, and achieve brand-name recognition without the traditional techniques of television advertising or much press coverage.

The media formats that shaped presidential races over the past thirty years have not exactly disappeared. The smart politician still wants exposure on CBS and in newspapers and magazines. But alongside the now-traditional structure, a new somewhat crazy house of mirrors has developed—the pop/interactive media. To his credit, President Clinton has been pragmatic about using the new structures to build support in his first three years in the White House. Over the past two decades, the number of people telling the public opinion pollsters that they are angry and alienated has steadily increased. From the Vietnam tragedy through the Watergate follies to the savings and loan bailout, Americans have been given good reason to hate the political culture. Clinton would have been foolish not to use as many means as possible to reach turned-off voters. As Lyndon Johnson advised, you have to go hunting where the ducks are. These days the voters are just as likely to be listening to A.M. drive-time radio as reading the *New York Times;* indeed, when voters climb into their cars for the morning commute, there is no contest between the two formats.

The old-media screening committee was not happy about a process that attempted to go over its head by talking directly to the audience. A wonderful implosion of the pre-TV days, the traditional, and the new populist forms occurred during the 1992 campaign. Old newsworthy David Broder made one of his regular appearances on CNN (new news) to deplore the "excesses" of postmodern media politics (future news). Broder recalled with visible nostalgia that back in 1960, in the good old days before television of any kind, network or cable, was a factor in the Democratic Party primaries, John F. Kennedy had to face real contests in only two states, West Virginia and Wisconsin. Democratic Party regulars, such as Richard J. Daley of Chicago and David Lawrence of Pennsylvania, could be counted on to deliver the major delegate blocs. But then television and big media took control of the primaries from the parties; or rather, the changes instituted by the Democratic Party in 1972 made this takeover possible—all in the cause of reform and popular democracy. Now, to hear the screening committee complain, it misses the rowdy machine bosses it once excluded from the Club.

The old lines dividing insider and outsider, politics and entertainment, news and talk, have not been blurred as much as they have been obliterated. In 1988, the Reverend Jesse Jackson was a serious candidate for president; in 1992, he was a news commentator on CNN. At screen-right facing commentator Jackson was John Sununu, the former White House chief of staff under George Bush. Sununu, in turn, had gotten his position as a commentator for CNN when the previous noisy occupant, Pat Buchanan, exited CNN to run for president. Rejected in every race he ran, Buchanan dropped out of the competition . . . to reclaim his pundit's chair at CNN. There he began preparing his campaign for 1996. Media, in fact, has become a last refuge for the discarded politician. Defeated in his bid to be reelected governor of New York for a fourth term, Mario Cuomo won a slot on talk radio. In Chicago, the longtime alderman, county chairman, and failed mayoral candidate Edward Vrdolyak became the co-host of an afternoon call-in show on WLS radio. Jerry Brown, former governor and presidential candidate, reappeared as the host of a syndicated, two-hour, Monday–Friday radio call-in show, *We the People with Jerry Brown.* Jerry Springer topped them all; the former mayor of Cincinnati has his own *national* TV talk show. A multipage spread in *People* magazine certified his celebrityhood. News-entertainment, politics-talk show, party leader-media host: the parts became interchangeable.[2]

As we shall see, the advent of pop campaigning, talk shows, and interactive media formats contributed to changing presidential politics in the 1990s, for better *and* worse. In the process, they also helped puncture some of the growing mythology about news coverage and political communications. One of the sillier academic safaris of the 1980s explored television coverage of presidential campaigns and decided that they were "information poor." Researchers at Harvard and the University of California, among other earnest notetakers, concluded that presidential campaigns had been reduced to mere sound bites on the evening news. One widely quoted study reported that in 1968, excerpts from the candidate's daily speech used on the evening news were on average twenty-three seconds long; by 1988, the excerpts were averaging less than ten seconds, and still shrinking. The research, however, was suspect to start with, since it included in its measurements what television producers call "natural sound." Thus, if George Bush was shown saying, "Hi, how are you?", the three seconds were counted in the survey. "Of course, those numbers made us look like fools," Susan Zirinsky, political editor of *CBS News,* told us.

No sooner had the researchers pulled the last page of this news from their computer printers than the 1992 sound-bite campaign turned into the sound-*glut* campaign. By the late spring of 1992, viewers could not get away from the candidates—morning, noon, early evening, or late night. In one sample period we studied during the last two weeks of June, the electorate's audio circuits suffered from an overload of sound. We counted: extended monologues from the standard stump speeches of Bush, Clinton, and Perot on the *NBC Nightly News* for three nights running; forty minutes of George and Barbara Bush with Barbara Walters on ABC's *20/20,* followed by a one-hour interview with George Bush on *CBS This Morning;* an hour of Bill Clinton on NBC's *Today* show (his second such appearance in two months), as well as Clinton's breakfast chat with the folks at ABC's *Good Morning America;* wall-to-wall Perot for the better part of one hour on the *Today* show (for a second time) and Perot twanging away twice in one night on ABC, first as the subject of a Peter Jennings's one-hour report and then as Jennings's guest, together with a studio audience, on an expanded ninety-minute edition of *Nightline.* All of that sound glut occurred a full seventeen weeks before the election.

By the fall campaign, some voters might have welcomed a few seconds of natural sound. They did not get many. In the period from September 1 to October 19, the candidates and their running mates logged no fewer than thirty-nine sit-down appearances on Larry King, the morning programs, public television, cable, and the call-in shows—plus the six hours of the candidates' debate-time appearances. "The voters are getting ample opportunity to hear the candidates," a bemused Jennings told us.

The complaint that presidential campaigning has become less "serious" is harder to dismiss than the sound-bite myth. Candidates have always played to the audience, elites and the groundlings (those with the vote, anyway). Something *was* lost when the campaign migrated from the old, hard-news formats to the once-over-easy talk shows, presided over by buttery hosts. "Larry King is not a journalist, as he is quick to admit, but an interviewer," the *New York Times* explained, as if talking to a not-too-bright child. By choosing to appear on talk shows and viewer call-ins, the candidates, in theory, circumvented the scrutiny of journalists armed with tough questions and knowledgeable follow-ups. But viewers who watched Tabitha Soren and her MTV studio audience quiz candidate Clinton came away with mixed feelings about the civilian interrogators, for sometimes their questions were as good as those posed by journalists.

Typically, newshounds operate with an up-to-date "data bank"—they know what news is being played on page one and at the top of the evening news. That is, they know what is on *their* minds. "Civilian" questions are less timely, less wonkish, more emotional. Still, it was a White House correspondent who asked Bush the terminally sappy question, "What would you say to Perot if you met him on the street?" Viewers first became aware of this gap between the journalists' and the civilians' world during the New Hampshire primaries, when the "professionals" were asking Clinton about Gennifer Flowers while the voters wanted to know how his economic proposals might affect their state.

Some facts are not in dispute. There is more product available to process and more channel space to be filled. Politics is now more accessible, if not more substantial. Politicians have become more talkative: there can never be a "Silent Cal" again, in part because the candidates have put themselves in talk-show situations where they must produce longer, fuller responses to questions. By the time the Bush-Clinton-Perot campaign was over, no one could complain that "all we heard were sound bites." Peter Jennings affirmed as much when he told us, "We got better material for our evening news stories from the candidates' call-ins than we did in the old days, when you had to grab them for a quote as their motorcade headed over the bridge to some street rally in Brooklyn."

With the differences blurred between the civilian callers and the "professionals," between the Tabitha Sorens and the Maria Shrivers, soft news and hard news began to resemble each other. News has always been a part of the popular culture, yet still somehow separate; feet stuck in the muddled passions and actions of the real world, head straining for knowledge and clarity. Anyone who has done serious, sustained newswork understands that "objectivity" is a myth; he or she also understands that some myths are useful. The pretentiousness of "political journalism" is easy to mock; but the desire to be, for lack of a better word, a truth teller, rather than an entertainment figure, is more than admirable: it is essential.

From the point of view of ordinary consumers, however, Peter Jennings and Larry King—and David Broder and Pat Buchanan—belong to the same common crew that comes into their homes on the TV or the radio. The consumers' blithe confusion is understandable. The serious journalists coexist side by side with the rude entertainers in the marketplace of prime time and the newsstand racks, competing for stories and the audience's attention. This proximity of the serious and the antic breeds more than competition. When one sneezes, the other catches cold, and so the virus has spread in the last few years. The fastest-growing category on television over the past five years is the tabloid magazine show, such as *A Current Affair, Hard Copy,* and *Inside Edition* (the rock-'em, sock-'em titles announce their intentions). "The entire news establishment has been affected by the new 'informational' shows," Peter Jennings acknowledged, choosing his words carefully as befits one of the high priests of the old order. The establishment still tries to keep its distance in the new tabloid environment, but only by a few degrees of separation. All three network evening news programs gave ample attention over a two-week period to the saga on ice of Olympic skaters Nancy Kerrigan and Tonya Harding. According to Jennings, "We did Tonya but we didn't lead with her"—the anchor version of the old brothel line, "I'll have a drink but I won't go upstairs."

The newcomers to the neighborhood are a raucous lot. Some are mean spirited, and some are slobs, purposefully so, dumping their garbage out onto the common spaces of the media village. Like charismatic political leaders of an earlier era, the new crowd pleasers have loyal followings. When 8 million book buyers made the writings of Rush Limbaugh and Howard Stern, respectively, the nation's number-one and number-two best-selling hardcovers in the winter of 1993–94, the tweedy classes began to pay attention. Political candidates and elected officials ignore the formats of electronic populism at their own risk. During the 1992 campaign, when candidate Clinton appeared on morning drive time in New York with Don Imus, a star of talk radio, careful listeners could track the evolution of the successful Clintonian image. In his Imus appearance, Clinton shunned his too-plausible, lawyerlike pronouncements—a style designed to play to the old media. Instead, he used humor and a lot of self-deprecation, getting down with the irreverent Imus. Explaining his saxophone-playing technique to Imus, Clinton said that he does not inhale, satirizing his own earlier, credulity-straining, lawyerly dodge about his past use of marijuana. By staying in that populist mode and reaching the audience directly, without the intercession of a querulous press, Clinton won points with Imus and with the host's morning drive-time listeners.[3] Later, Clinton learned how to make that aw-shucks persona play nationally, in a variety of direct-media formats. The Clinton show went on to Washington in January 1993.

The neighborhood hardly quieted down. Talk noise grew louder—one consequence of the permanent campaign. The Clinton administration's starts and stops during its first three years in office provided hours of drive-time materials for a chorus of gleeful radio and television squawkers: the continuation of the election campaign by other means.

Historically, candidates have searched for a potent "silver bullet"—the ringing slogan, political positioning, or incisive strategy—that slays the opposition. Silicon Valley's high-technologists seek the same power in their marketplace; the currently fashionable phrase they use is "killer app," the application that makes consumers want to buy the product. Today, the formats for political communications are new; but the efforts by Clinton and his opponents to reach the electorate directly with their killer app, and win dominant market share without the mediation of the established press, grow out of an old and familiar impulse.

"Nobody Here But Just Us Folks"

Time after time . . . I have taken an issue directly to the voter by radio, and invariably I have met a most heartening response.
—Franklin Delano Roosevelt

Political leaders have adopted new modes of communication to advance themselves and their policies across two centuries of American history. The aim, then as now, has been to bypass their critics—with traditional media, like newspapers, came scrutiny—and reach the public with as much of their message intact as possible. The use of alternative media formats helped "agitators" like Thomas Paine bring their words to the desired audience without journalist intermediaries. Paine's pamphlets were produced on hand presses in print shops, the Kinko's of his day. "Common Sense," distributed in 1776, and the series "The Crisis" (1776–83) promoted independence for the colonies. Tellingly, Paine's writing style was noted for its plain, colloquial, rhetoric-free prose. Paine said he abhorred "high-toned exclamation." Alive and agitating today, he would have taken his case for resistance to England to the TV talk shows and radio call-ins.

A few years later, when the framers of the Constitution sought acceptance for their new document while trying to turn public support away from the Articles of Confederation, they utilized the pamphlet form as well. The "Federalist Papers" of James Madison, John Jay, and Alexander Hamilton stand as an early example of direct political appeal to the electorate. Because the antifederalists were most vocal in New York, the three published their pamphlets there; today, political time buyers choose similar "battleground states," where victory is essential, to mount multimillion dollar television advertising campaigns. The "Federalist Papers" were masterfully written, effectively selling the Constitution to the public, sketching the dangers of self-interest and factions, explaining how the Constitution would insure a functioning society without infringing on personal rights. The best speechwriters today still try to emulate the authors' clear, closely reasoned rhetoric.

The Constitution was promoted as a way to ensure central control over violent factions, such as the one that led to Shays's Rebellion. (In August 1786, a group of debt-ridden Massachusetts farmers organized by Daniel Shays launched an armed insurrection against the state and its courts, seeking to halt foreclosures on property mortgages and their own imprisonment for tax debts.) The authors of the "Federalist Papers" were quick to play the fear card, addressing both the public's economic anxieties and worries about civil strife (not unlike Ross Perot's tactics when he attempted to rally support against the North American Free Trade Agreement [NAFTA] in 1993).

The "Federalist Papers" were aimed at a limited audience: adult white males who qualified as voters because they owned property and could read. In the 1850s, Abraham Lincoln and Stephen A. Douglas took politics on the road to reach listeners of all classes and levels of literacy. Lincoln challenged Douglas to a series of formal debates across Illinois. At stake was an Illinois senate seat, but "Honest Abe" was shrewd enough to grasp that his personal road to Washington led out to the people and back again. The two men disagreed on whether the western territories, when admitted to the union, should be "slave" or "free." Douglas supported the right of each new state to choose for itself. Lincoln opposed the institution of slavery (he had been pushed—"radicalized on race," we would say today—by his law partner George Herndon). The traveling Lincoln-Douglas show enabled potential voters in remote locations to hear the arguments firsthand. The candidates reached the audience directly, and not by way of highly partisan newspaper accounts. Illiterate voters, in any case, had no alternative except to listen. The taller Lincoln's stage presence, as much as his arguments, ensured victory in both the debates and the popular election. He still lost the senatorial seat to Douglas, however; the state legislature had final responsibility for choosing state senators, and it was not swayed by Lincoln's oratory. (The Republican Party leadership though was, and it gave him his party's presidential nomination in 1860.)

For the next sixty years, candidates campaigned and presidents presided as they had in the previous sixty-odd years of the republic. Then came radio, a direct-market technology that brought leaders into unmediated intimacy with the citizenry. No longer did voters have to go to the train station or the town square to participate in the political process; the process came to them. Woodrow Wilson was the first president to attempt to reach a radio audience. Burdened by flagging health, Wilson turned to the new medium for his final campaign, seeking Americans' support for U.S. membership in the League of Nations. His speech was a failure. The radio sets at the time were primitive contraptions. Unregulated stations often broadcast at the same time on the same frequency, and Wilson's words were drowned out by interference. (The chaotic state of the airways lasted until the Federal Radio Commission was established by Congress in 1926.) Warren Harding had better luck. He was the first president to deliver a speech via radio and actually be heard. His topic was the World Court; the broadcast was carried by radio station KSD in St. Louis on June 21, 1923. Harding's words also were aired simultaneously on WEAF in New York, relayed via long-distance telephone lines. When Harding began speaking on KSD, other radio stations went silent, in deference to presidential authority and to the importance attached to the topic.

In its first decades, the new medium reached only a tiny audience; 1920s sets were expensive, costing $150 (the equivalent of $1,000 today). But radio had *status:* it was no accident that the fledgling NBC network sponsored the NBC Symphony Orchestra, and that the musicians all wore evening clothes when they performed in the New York studio. Thus, even though Harding was a plodder in many matters, he was politically savvy enough to see the potential of a new means to reach the voters directly. Campaigning for the World Court, he relied on tradition—a tour by railroad train—and technology. He had his private coach equipped with a radio transmitter so he could reach out to larger audiences beyond the whistle stops.

In the 1920s, as in the 1990s, people needed a reason for listening; radio had to become special, with a social resonance beyond the technological appeal of its novelty. Stars from the entertainment world, such as Arturo Toscanini of the NBC Symphony Orchestra, as well as popular comedians, provided some early identity; but the first real radio voice emerged from politics.

Both the Democratic and Republican national conventions were broadcast live in the summer of 1924. At the time, there were some 3 million American households with radio sets. The radio audience tuned to the Democratic convention heard an appealing politician from New York, Franklin Delano Roosevelt, give one of the speeches nominating Al Smith, the governor of New York. Roosevelt's listeners liked what they heard. (Forty years later, a strong speech nominating Barry Goldwater and the Republican convention conferred national political status on a middle-aged former actor named Ronald Reagan.) Smith lost to Calvin Coolidge in 1924 and then to Herbert Hoover in 1928. But the Democrat had the surer grasp of the new radio medium. "Tonight

I am no⟨...⟩ ⟨...⟩nds of people in a great hall," Smith told radio list⟨...⟩ ⟨...⟩re the 1928 election, sounding uncannily like the fireside chats that were to be given by FDR a few years later. "I am going to take this opportunity to talk intimately to my radio audience alone, as though I were sitting with you in your own home and personally discussing with you the decision that you are to make tomorrow."

Roosevelt listened and learned. In 1932, he became the first presidential candidate to accept his party's nomination on nationwide radio, live from the Democratic convention in Chicago. Radio, he reasoned, could be used to bring the event directly into the homes of listeners in a way that was both personal and presidential, while bypassing the traditional newspaper channels. The fact that four out of five newspapers in the country were traditionally Republican at election time made radio doubly attractive. The acceptance speech required some scheming, because FDR was not in Chicago at the time of his nomination. Tradition demanded that the nominee stay away from the convention and signify acceptance when called upon by party officials a few days later, after the convention was over. Roosevelt understood the importance of public ceremony, however; as soon as he learned of his nomination—by radio—he telephoned party officials inside Chicago Stadium and requested that the convention remain in session long enough for him to arrive by plane. Once in Chicago, FDR made both political and radio history by reaching out to the stadium throng as well as to a growing listening public, and pledging himself to "a new deal."

FDR solidified his personal relationship with the Great Depression audience on March 12, 1933, just days after his inauguration, when he used radio time to raise the spirits of listeners and build support for his plan to reopen the nation's banks. His speech, broadcast on both CBS and NBC, reached most of the 17 million radio sets then in homes; this was one of the largest audiences in the history of the new medium. Once in touch with the electorate,

Roosevelt nurtured his advantage through no fewer than twenty fireside chats, which averaged a little over half an hour each. He was confined to a wheelchair through four campaigns and four terms as president, a victim of polio. Few in the audience could keep in mind his physical impairment; *listening* to him, they heard only the strong voice. (The newspapers, with one or two notorious exceptions, abstained by an implicit "gentlemen's agreement" from discussing his polio or showing photographs of the wheelchair, the iron braces, or the withered legs.) Most Americans knew only the official above-the-waist FDR: confident grin, jaunty cigarette holder, and reassuring radio presence. If radio had not existed, it might have been necessary for the Roosevelt White House to invent it.

Long before the radio and television call-in shows, FDR urged the audience to write in and express its opinions to those in Washington. "Tell me your troubles," he said in one of his first fireside chats. The public took him at his word. For a time, as many as 6,500 letters a day were coming into the White House. When giving his chats, FDR would look at a blank wall and try to "visualize" the audience: the same preparation television presenters are encouraged to make today.[1]

The conservative press's instant analysis of the fireside chats was predictably negative. Newspaper columnists likened FDR's radio appeals to Stalin's purges in communist Russia. The attacks only increased his enthusiasm for the press's rival medium. At one point, he gave some thought to creating a government radio network, to broadcast reports on livestock, agriculture, and the weather—and perhaps his own political speeches. Popular fears of "statism," stoked by editorial-page commentary, and the physical limits of the radio spectrum killed this early version of a C-SPAN-style channel. Then as now, FDR's use of radio in his reelection campaigns prompted complaints about the advantages of incumbency; in 1936 both KECA and KFI radio in Los Angeles refused to carry an FDR fireside chat, on the grounds that he was giving a political speech. Radio was no longer a technological toy. FDR joked that he would become a radio commentator after he retired, and his audience laughed knowingly: he was already a superstar of the medium.

The Roosevelt-haters had their answer to the fireside chats in the weekly radio sermons of the Roman Catholic priest, Charles E. Coughlin. Father Coughlin used his pulpit at the Shrine of the Little Flower church to catapult himself onto local midwestern radio in the late 1920s. By 1930 he was reaching millions of listeners on the CBS radio network. In November 1934, sixty years before the electronic populism of Ross Perot, Coughlin used radio to form the National Union for Social Justice, "an articulate, organized lobby of the people to bring united pressure upon the representatives at Washington for the purpose of securing the passage of laws which we want passed."[2]

By the 1940s, radio had secured its place alongside print as a political medium, reaching people emotionally and giving listeners a sense of participation: You Are There. On December 8, 1941, an estimated 60 million people heard Roosevelt denounce the Japanese attack on Pearl Harbor as a "day of infamy" and ask Congress for a declaration of war against the Axis powers. By D Day, June 6, 1944, when radio brought the news of the allied invasion of Europe, there were more than 48 million radio sets in the United States, one for every two Americans. When the popular artist Norman Rockwell memorialized the home front on invasion day as he wanted it remembered, he painted three listeners gathered around the radio in a luncheonette. A generation later, the picture would have to be redrawn to incorporate the new medium of television.

Television no more "replaced" radio in the 1950s than radio had "replaced" newspapers or magazines in the 1930s—or, to continue the parallels, no more than television will be supplanted by specialized on-demand cable channels and online computer networks in the 1990s. After the hyperventilating about "revolutionary media" subsides, Gutenberg still will coexist with the Internet. New media are additive; they increase the consumers' options, rather than subtract from them. Selective consumers have usually adjusted their tastes and habits to fit in a new medium, when its price was deemed reasonable, its technology more convenient than daunting, and the product enjoyable and/or useful.

While FDR was the first president to appear on television (at the RCA exhibit at the 1939 World's Fair in New York), his successors were the ones who embraced the improving technology. Initially, presidents approached television cautiously; diffidence yielded to pursuit, however, as successive White Houses grasped that television was where the voters were. In 1950, Harry S Truman allowed CBS News's television cameras to film a cabinet meeting in the White House. Truman's successor, Dwight D. Eisenhower, permitted filming of a similar meeting three years later, to show that Republicans were not afraid of the television camera. There was less than met the eye in Ike's apparent openness; his cabinet officers had been well rehearsed and their comments carefully scripted in advance by the copywriting wizards of the BBDO advertising agency, then the hot shop on Madison Avenue.

The changes in American presidential politics brought about by the new medium of television were demonstrated most vividly by the transformation of election-eve campaigning. For decades, the election-eve rally was an American political ritual, a symbol of the way the candidates and the electorate wanted to regard each other. Pre-TV, election eve meant climactic torchlight parades, fireworks displays, and rallies of the party faithful. The party mobilized voters already committed to its ticket and the candidates were emotionally energized by the pulsing crowd. The direct contact made the months of campaigning worthwhile. But the reach of television enabled the candidates to achieve something more practical than a mutual emotional support group at a parade. Millions of voters, including those not yet committed, could hear and see a final appeal. From the first, election-eve TV events were arranged to make the key undecided groups a part of the show.

"Good evening, folks!" General Dwight D. Eisenhower said, sitting in a Boston hotel room together with his wife Mamie, Senator Richard M. Nixon, Nixon's wife Pat, and a 35 mm camera. It was Monday, November 3, 1952. Election eve, as well as the rest of the electoral process, had moved indoors into the nation's living rooms. In place of 15,000 party faithful assembled in a town square or Madison Square Garden to hear their candidate, the new election eves eventually would attract audiences of 150 million viewers, rallying around their living room television sets.

The evolving styles of the candidates' election-eve broadcasts from the 1950s to the 1990s reveal the distance both television and politics have traveled together.[3] These images also suggest what has endured for the candidates and the voters. It is very easy to forget how, every four years in America, political power is magisterially reaffirmed or transferred, without tanks in the streets or the disaffection of the factions that Hamilton et al. worried about. On election eve, both the candidates and television—their chosen means of communication—have tried to rise to the occasion, in part by inviting the audience's participation.

The image of the Eisenhowers and the Nixons sitting stiffly in hotel chairs seems as quaint today as the general's greeting to the audience about to watch the broadcast. Yet, for all the 1990s talk about cyberspace and two-way media, the Eisenhower-Nixon ticket "went interactive" in 1952, when the two candidates settled in to listen to voters for the next hour. Instead of the candidates addressing their supporters, the supporters addressed the candidates with their comments and concerns.

The Eisenhowers and the Nixons, the audience was told, would be seeing the show along with the viewers at home. "In that way we all get to be together, almost in your living rooms,"

Eisenhower explained. And so the 1952 TV audience watched the candidates watching their small, boxy, black-and-white set. The program bore the look of 1950s TV and its gee-whiz infatuation with technology. The camera went "hopscotching" around the country. From Chicago, Hollywood, Baltimore, San Francisco, Minneapolis, and other breathtaking stops, Republican supporters "report to the General." Eisenhower listened to army veterans, farmers, factory workers, students, immigrants, African-Americans—and John Wayne. Looking uncomfortable, actor Wayne ticked off a list of Eisenhower's Hollywood supporters, including Fred Astaire, Gary Cooper, Bing Crosby, Abbott and Costello, and Amos and Andy: the cultural elite of the movie business in the early 1950s. Back in Boston at the end of the program, as the transmission faded to black, viewers heard Mamie Eisenhower say to her husband: "Let's get home to our grandchildren." The words sounded heartfelt and unrehearsed.

Adlai E. Stevenson, the 1952 Democratic candidate, and his running mate, Senator John Sparkman from Alabama, chose a more formal TV setting; they were seen seated together at a desk chatting, with their families standing awkwardly in the background. Stevenson asked his son Gordy what he thought of the campaign. In a quaking voice, the son replied: "Well, if the strong feeling for you by the universities is any indication of your national strength, I'd say you're in." His father laughed hollowly, prompting the son to add: "I hope." "You hope!" exclaimed the candidate. The small talk over, Stevenson addressed the voters. He has, he said, "talked sense to the American people . . . Win or lose, I have told you the truth as I see it. I have said what I meant and meant what I said." As Stevenson reached the peroration of his well-crafted speech, the TV sound faded. The chitchat with his son and Sparkman went on too long; Stevenson had run out of air time. His campaign also came up short; the next day, the Republican ticket carried thirty-nine states.

By the 1960s, the candidates had learned about time cues. Their advertising teams and television-trained producers also brought more edge to the candidates' climactic appeals, in keeping with the grim events of a decade that included the unwinnable war in Vietnam, the assassinations of the Kennedys and Martin Luther King, and urban riots in a dozen big cities. In 1964, for example, the Lyndon Johnson forces wanted to plant firmly in the TV audience's mind the image of an "unstable" Barry Goldwater, a man supposedly eager to wage nuclear war. The Johnson media people produced "Daisy," a thirty-second political spot and followed it with a half-hour program called "Sorry, Senator Goldwater. We Just Can't Risk It." In it, a panel of military and academic brass treated Goldwater as a kind of Dr. Strangelove. "It was one long 'Daisy' spot. We said, in effect, if Goldwater's elected, he'll blow up the world," recalled David Garth, then a thirty-four-year-old TV producer for the Democrats.[4] Johnson led Goldwater by a wide margin in the polls throughout the campaign, and so the final overkill was LBJ's. "True, he didn't need the program," Garth acknowledged when we interviewed him three decades later. "But you always have to run scared."

The 1960s and the Vietnam War created the notorious "credibility gap" for candidates. Voters' distrust of elected officials, and of all authority, was high. It became essential that the candidates and their election-eve TV programs appeared to be free of all artifice. Richard Nixon's producers responded in 1968 with an elaborately "unslick" broadcast format that artfully concealed its real off-camera slickness. The comic Jackie Gleason, pale and puffy looking, but at the height of his popularity, introduced Nixon, who explained the plan for the show. Viewers could call a Los Angeles telephone number that flashed periodically on the screen. "[Our] tremendous bank of girls" on stage would write out the questions. Then, Nixon said, another group of "girls," called the "Nixonaires," would carry the questions to Oklahoma football coach Bud Wilkinson, the interlocutor. The "Nixonaires" were airline stewardesses dressed in short skirts and jockey caps. Later, the writer Joe McGinniss reported that the questions were reworded backstage before going to Wilkinson (the Nixon people denied the claim). In any case, no questioner played hardball. A caller asked about Eisenhower's health; Nixon cheerily reported that Mrs. Eisenhower "told me that he's living for just two things—one, he wants to live to see us win the election, and he wants to attend the marriage" of his grandson David to Nixon's daughter Julie. Nixon answered questions on live TV for two hours, and then repeated a similar program for a West Coast broadcast. Advisers had argued against the effort, but the candidate, haunted by his narrow loss to John F. Kennedy in 1960, was adamant. "It was my best campaign decision," he wrote in his memoirs. "Had we not had that last telethon, I believe Humphrey would have squeaked through with a close win on election day."

The Democrats' election-eve effort on behalf of candidate Hubert Humphrey resembled Nixon's in many respects. It was on for two hours in prime time and it was carried live. Another two-hour show was done for the West Coast, and a group of attractive young women was on hand to take callers' questions. There were, however, differences. The Humphrey telethon boasted such celebrities as Paul Newman, Johnny Carson, Frank Sinatra, Bill Cosby, Edward G. Robinson, and Burt Lancaster. The stars answered some calls and then read out the questions. The set was supposed to look "authentic." TV cables snaked all over, the floor was littered with coffee cups, "just like a real telethon," remembered producer Bob Squier. When Squier discovered that "some efficient person from ABC" had straightened up just before airtime, he hurriedly restored the disarray—counterprogramming against Nixonian neatness.[5]

In the 1970s, slick production values and cinematic techniques remolded the election-eve presentations, enhancing the appeal of the program as spectacle. Nine out of every ten U.S. households now had at least one television set, most likely with color. Election-eve shows began delivering less unscripted talk and more bright pictures. In 1972, Nixon was confined to a four-minute address; then the show moved on to a documentary-style film of the president at work in the grandeur of the Oval Office. Nixon earnestly discussed such topics as education and revenue sharing with an aide. Pop elements were introduced by the use of Madison Avenue-type "product" testimonials; instead of celebrity endorsers, the White House staff sang Nixon's praises. Viewers heard from the president's doctor ("he thrives on work") and Henry Kissinger ("there's a certain heroic quality about how he conducts his business").

Opponent George McGovern conducted a doomed campaign, but presented the most emotional election-eve special of any decade. Soft-voiced actor David Wayne narrated the program, which was produced and directed by the acclaimed documentary filmmaker Charles Guggenheim. The images could have played at an art-film festival: McGovern and his handsome family walking through woods . . . cut to grim, muddy American soldiers . . . cut to Vietnamese children crying . . . cut to the candidate listening to the stories of a group of wheelchair-bound Vietnam vets in a VA hospital as the handheld camera eavesdrops, cinema verité style.[6]

Four years later, candidates Gerald Ford and Jimmy Carter tried to lighten things up a little. In the first election eve after Vietnam and Watergate, Ford's media people wanted to get voters' minds as far *away* from Washington politics as possible. The Ford election-eve show began with the former major league baseball player Joe Garagiola aboard Air Force One. Viewers were made to feel like the jet had just taken off from Andrews Air Force Base and was physically removing itself from the capital, heading West to the "real America." The affable Garagiola was seen shouting to make himself heard. He began by promising a film about Ford. But first, he said, "somebody else has something to say about this election and about this man . . . . It's Pearlie! Miss Pearl Bailey!" At this point, the camera turned to the African-American singer sitting on a couch, addressing the TV audience. It took her a while to work up to praising Ford: ". . . Oh, he's made some mistakes, honey! You better believe he has! I wouldn't sit here and even try to say he didn't. But I'll tell you what . . . he has something I like very much in every human being, simplicity and honesty, 'cause I really believe he's an honest man—that's why I like Gerald Ford." Cut back to Garagiola: "That's a real lady," he said. "Gives you a lump in your throat."

Jimmy Carter tried a combination of 1950s Ike-style interactive folksiness and 1960s Nixon-Humphrey audience call-ins. His finale featured everyday citizens on film with their questions. Carter sometimes referred to the questioner by name ("Well, I want to answer Bob Gary's question first"). He worked in the fact that "my mother Lillian is 78 years old" and so he will never forget "about the special problems of the elderly people of this country." A Hispanic man's question evoked a reply from Naval Academy-graduate Carter in Spanish as the screen provided English-language subtitles.

Election eves in the 1980s were dominated by Ronald Reagan. Aware of some public unease about the candidate's Hollywood-actor roots, the Reagan media team cast against type, as they say in the film industry. The 1980 Reagan election-eve show was austere. Reagan addressed the camera directly; there was no biographical film, no endorsers, no genial hosts or chorus, no family members, no artifice. Only his running mate, George Bush, was at his side. And one other presence. "Last year, I lost a friend who was more than a symbol of the Hollywood dream industry . . ." Reagan said. "John Wayne . . . did not believe that our country was ready for the dustbin of history, and if we just think about it, we too will know it isn't."

Like the spectral Wayne, certain other images reappear in election-eve specials of the last forty years, and the narrative subtexts remain remarkably constant. For example, the shows like to pause over the candidate's humble roots: "He was born and reared in modest surroundings. Many of us would feel at home in Ike's boyhood room," the announcer said in 1952. In 1972, White House aide John Ehrlichman confided that his boss, Richard Nixon, had an impoverished boyhood. In 1988, the patrician New Englander, George Herbert Walker Bush, also log-cabinized his history, telling the living-room audience about how, after World War II, he moved his young family to Texas, with "one room for the three of us." The biography omitted the fact that young Bush had gone to Texas to enter the oil business. The programs also like to emphasize that, for all the candidate has achieved, he has not lost the common touch. He's "one of the people," only more so. The 1956 announcer spoke of "just plain Ike—husband, father, grandfather, a warm human individual much like you yourself." In his 1972 film, Nixon played the piano. Carter's 1976 show opened with an exterior shot of his Plains, Georgia, home, with daughter Amy's bicycle propped against a tree. Most of all, the candidate is shown to be a devoted family man, sending the audience a subliminal message: he's like you (or more precisely, he's much like the median TV viewer who votes). "Even as you and I, Ike shared with Mrs. Eisenhower the satisfaction of becoming grandparents," said the announcer in 1952—the same year Stevenson was shown chatting amiably with his sons on live TV. Later films told viewers that familial love is President Nixon's "greatest private joy," that "Gerald and Betty Ford are a love story," and that, in the view of President Bush's son George, his father is "probably the most thoughtful man I know." The 1988 Bush biographical film reruns footage of the candidate picking up and kissing his youngest granddaughter.

A few election-eve shows feature rough stuff, though usually not as tough as "Daisy" and Dr. Strangelove in 1964. Stevenson in 1956 referred to Eisenhower's health problems—he suffered a heart attack and ileitis in the White House—and predicted that a Republican victory would put Richard Nixon in the Oval Office within four years ("I recoil at the prospect," said the fastidious Stevenson). In Eisenhower's show, announcer John Cameron Swayze replied obliquely: "I think you'll have to admit that the President looks even better at the end of this campaign than he did when he finished the campaign of '52." More often, the election-eve attacks are not that direct. In a veiled reference to Stevenson's divorce, the script for Ike's 1956 program made use of an outsider, an elderly African-American woman, who told the president: "Your devotion to Mrs. Eisenhower, [to] family life, can well be an example to the American home, the American youth."

Whatever their message, the natural question is, do such election-eve programs, with their calculated "just folks" formats, actually sway some voters? Probably yes, although the operative word is "some." "There's always a group of undecideds on the very last night," Bob Squier told us. "They feel that they have a patriotic obligation to vote, but they can't figure out which one to go for. On that last night you have one more opportunity to answer their questions." As David Garth says, a candidate ahead in the polls can never feel too sure.

In the end, the best of the final-night living-room exchanges remain art, not life. The most potent television images cannot make voters forget what happened in the weeks and months outside in the real world. The day after Charles Guggenheim's eloquent 1972 election-eve film for George McGovern was broadcast, the Democratic ticket lost forty-nine states; McGovern won only Massachusetts and the District of Columbia. Twenty years and five presidential elections later, the Democratic candidate Bill Clinton fared better on election day. His campaign had benefited not so much from art but from reality, specifically the Republicans' economic and social record in the previous four years under the indecisive Bush. The Clinton political consultant James Carville, who wore blue jeans and a sweatshirt and carefully nurtured his media persona of "colorful character," printed a sign for the campaign headquarters in Little Rock. "It's the Economy, Stupid," it read, a reminder for the staff that elections were about matters of substance and that they needed to "stay on message."

Once in the White House, however, the Clintonites became caught up in the new technology of political communications. Excited by all of the bright hardware, they lost sight of what mattered most: content, message, the software.

The Nerd Revolution

When *Rolling Stone* magazine assigned gonzo journalist Hunter S. Thompson to "cover" the 1972 presidential campaign, the editors prudently hired a young Harvard graduate named Timothy Crouse to keep Thompson on track. Crouse did more than make sure that the magazine's bar bills were paid and that its correspondent—the model for the macho "Duke" character in the comic strip "Doonesbury"—stayed out of jail. Crouse produced "The Boys on the Bus," an insightful study of the national press corps assigned to cover the George McGovern-Richard Nixon race. In the two decades since its publication, "The Boys on the Bus" has become a baseline for measuring both the performance of the campaign press and the shifting nature of political journalism. The 1972 press corps chronicled by Crouse was almost wholly white, male, and dumb, technologically speaking. Reporters carried manual typewriters and dictated their stories from telephone banks to home offices in 200- to 500-word segments (called "takes"). Once aboard the candidate's bus or plane, they were out of communication with their editors. When they composed their articles or television segments, they visualized an audience of consumer-voters very much like themselves.

By the time the presidential campaigns of the 1990s rolled around, the press corps had indisputably become the boys *and* girls on the bus. The Royal manuals had given way to laptop computers; complete stories were sent via modem directly to editors' computer screens. With everyone routinely equipped with cellular phones, reporters at any given time were never more than a beep away from the home office's beck and call. They were also much more attuned to the interests of readers and viewers, or more accurately, to the perceived *dis*interest of an audience considered largely apolitical and apathetic. These changes in the composition of the press corps and in the sophistication of their equipment cannot help but affect the content of the news being transmitted. The frat-house campaign bus was a metaphor for the old, insulated world of political journalism. The modern bus, inclusive, nerdy, instantly and interactively online, now travels into new political terrain.

The arrival of a significant number of women on the bus is quantitatively easy to document. Eight women reporters were mentioned in Crouse's book. Interestingly, the references were usually in a favorable context. According to Crouse, for example, "It was no coincidence that some of the toughest pieces on the 1972 Nixon campaign came from Sarah McClendon, Helen Thomas of UPI, Cassie Mackin of NBC, Marilyn Berger of the *Washington Post,* and Mary McGrory (from the now-departed *Washington Star).* They had always been outsiders. Having never been allowed to join in the cozy, clubby world of men, they had developed an uncompromising detachment and a bold independence of thought which often put the men to shame."[1] In 1992, a bus headcount by our News Study Group indicated that women made up one-fourth or more of the 100-plus working press corps members who regularly accompanied candidates George Bush and Bill Clinton on the campaign.[2] Some two dozen newspapers, TV and radio networks, magazines, and wire services assigned one or more women to prominent roles in their coverage. Twenty years later, too, there was less of the boys'-night-out behavior—the closing down of hotel bars, the too-cozy dealings with campaign staff, and the sexual playing around recorded by Crouse. Instead, an air of serious purpose filled the campaign busses, trains, planes, and computer-filing centers. "Everyone was more sober and better educated," said UPI correspondent Helen Thomas, who has covered the eight presidential campaigns since 1964. Clara Bingham, a twenty-nine-year-old *Newsweek* reporter assigned to her first presidential campaign in 1992, made the same point. "It was very nerdy," she said. "People are wedded to their tape recorders and computers." The political columnist Lars-Erik Nelson told us that in place of the sodden, bleary-eyed, night-prowling male journalists, he observed a lot of "New Man" behavior: not merely nerds in love with their laptops, but thoughtful "sensitive" husbands using their cellular phones to call home and wish their wives and children goodnight at bedtime.

More substantively, members of the abstemious campaign class of the 1990s produce qualitatively different coverage. Some of this difference can be attributed to the direct presence on board the bus of 1990s' women and model men—and their electronic gear. Some is explained by external factors, such as the broad demographic changes in the country since 1972 and the particular dynamics of recent elections.

The evidence for the "women's effect" on coverage over the last two decades is inevitably largely anecdotal. During the 1992 campaign, Jonathan Alter, the media columnist for *Newsweek*, subscribed to the Crouse notion that women frequently did better reporting than men. According to Alter, "part of this is because women are able to get interviewees to open up and talk more freely, saying things they might not say to a man . . . [there is] an intimacy between reporters and sources, and women seem to be more capable of handling intimacy." Our analysis of the newspaper and television stories in 1972 shows a pattern of attention to horserace coverage. The traditional journalists tracked which candidate was ahead in the key "battleground states." Such races were covered moment by moment (or inning by inning) as they "go down to the wire." In 1972, the early 1970s' cultural issues of "acid, abortion, and amnesty" were raised against McGovern. The Democratic Party was said to condone societywide permissiveness; but the subjects were not framed, for example, as questions of McGovern's individual lifestyle choice or his personal conscience. "The McGovern candidacy stood on one side of a 'cultural divide,'" remembered R. W. Apple, Jr., of the *New York Times*. "But the campaign did not personalize the issue. It was abstract." In the 1990s, by contrast, there has been more attention to personality and character—putatively "female" concerns—and marginally less abstract "male" sports talk and war imagery.

Apple was the quintessential 1972 bus insider, an authentic "Big Foot" in the journalistic patois. He played a more senior role in 1992, confining himself to strategic analysis and selective travel. One of his *Times* colleagues, Maureen Dowd, became a Big Foot, so prized by her editors that she could pick and choose her assignments. "Dowd isn't really interested in writing stories about who's ahead," Apple explained. "She is interested in giving the reader insight into why people behave the way they do." Apple suggested that Dowd's work is shaped by a generational perspective rather than by a "feminine sensibility." Dowd, he says, "has been interested most of her life in TV and movies, so you see in her writing allusions to popular culture." Dowd, speaking about her role in the campaign, picked her words carefully. "I'm in awe when people start to talk about the electoral map," she said. On the other hand, the traditional, male horserace handicappers like the columnists Jack Germond and Jules Witcover "aren't interested in the stories I like, which are much more—for lack of a better word—'human interest.' I like to do smaller features, humor, trends, sociological pieces. They want the baseball scores."

The women reporters on the bus split on the question of whether women actually bring different issues and different perspectives to their stories. Of the sixteen women we interviewed, nine thought there was a woman's effect (of a sort) on the 1992 coverage, while seven dismissed or downplayed the idea. On one side, Andrea Mitchell, the NBC News television reporter, said that "women correspondents have always been a little bit outside the inner circle at the White House, because most politicians are surrounded by male advisers." While male correspondents "bond" and "pal around with the staff," women remain outsiders; consequently, "there's less chance of us being co-opted . . . we're a little tougher and more adversarial in the best sense of the words." Two other women, both broadcasters who covered the candidates in the 1970s, suggested that women correspondents would not have gone along with the wink-and-nudge approach to public figures' sexual escapades the way male reporters did. "There would have been no Judith Exner secrets in the Kennedy White House if more women were there then," we were told.

On the other side, Helen Thomas argued against the notion of a special "women's take" on politics. "There is no question that women are more accepted," Thomas said. "But I don't think they've changed the campaign. They run as hard for the planes. They do the same job. I don't see any real difference in the coverage, and I don't think there is such a thing as the 'female story' in the overall campaign." Susan Feeney, thirty-one, of the *Dallas Morning News,* covered her second presidential campaign in 1992; like Thomas, she dismissed the idea of a "women's angle." "Maybe women are a little more sensitive to some things, but I don't think so," she said. "If you took all my stories for a year and put them alongside a male reporter's stories, I don't think you'd find they were vastly different."

When our News Study Group did a comparison of "male" and "female" approaches to one major running story—how Hillary Rodham Clinton has been portrayed in media accounts—we did see differences.[3] These differences reflect the internal politics of the editorial assignment process as much as any "gender consciousness." During the presidential primary season (January to July 1992), when the Hillary Clinton story was fresh and getting good display in the news pages and on the evening news, male reporters were more likely to be writing about Hillary Clinton than were female reporters. For example, in this "high-interest" period, we counted sixty-two stories with male bylines, fifty-eight with female bylines, and thirty unattributed. However, from the Democratic National Convention through the election and Inauguration Day, when Hillary Clinton was under the constricting supervision of her image advisers, and less likely to be making major news, women's bylines far outnumbered men's. Next, in the first year of the Clinton administration, when Hillary Clinton's health-care work increased her visibility and her newsworthiness, more male bylines appeared again.

The same was true during other "big stories" of the first Clinton term, such as the Whitewater land deal, the Republican electoral victory of November 1994, and the First 100 Days of the "Contract with America." The more "important" the news, the more likely the male byline. Further, when stories appeared in the main news sections of newspapers, the bylines were likely to be male (ninety-four to seventy-seven, in the case of news stories about health care). But if the story was deemed soft or featurized, it tended to be placed in the newspaper's inside pages in the style, living, or daily magazine sections. (Our sample included the *New York Times,* the *Washington Post,* the *Los Angeles Times,* the *Boston Globe,* and the *Chicago Tribune.*) And, once stories were placed in the feature sections, the bylines were four times more likely to be a woman's (forty-five to ten). All this suggests that some assignment and supervisory editors, who are still more likely to be male, are also still more likely to deal some of the "good stories" to male reporters.

The gender effect on content remains hard to demonstrate conclusively. Michelle McQueen, who left her job as a senior writer for the *Wall Street Journal* to join ABC News in 1992, adopts a mid-register analysis. She holds that reporters, male or female, do not create policy issues: the candidates and, most of all, the electorate, set agendas. "Abortion became a campaign issue," McQueen told us, "because voters on both sides, pro choice and pro life, made it an issue, and not because women were on the campaign bus." Although individual journalists may bring a high degree of interest or a certain level of intensity to the traveling press corps—appropriately, or why would they be hired?—"you could write stories all day long that won't resonate with the public until it recognizes something that matters to it." McQueen concluded that "campaign issues flow from the bottom up, not from the press bus or airplane down." But McQueen and half a dozen other reporters interviewed also acknowledged that when the press group is mixed, the dynamics change, and relationships shift.

The Clinton campaign press was different, say, from the Michael Dukakis group in 1988 (for one, there were the candidates' contrasting standings in the polls, and, of course, the outcomes). Similarly, the press contingent assigned to a challenger is not like the White House press corps. Typically, the latter behaves in a buttoned-down, self-important manner—in a word, "governmental." (Years ago, the humorist Russell Baker pointed out how journalists take on the coloration of their beat: State Department reporters dressing in pin-striped suits, Pentagon correspondents favoring bush jackets and other trig gear, etc.) Crouse, among other critics, recognized that the traveling press corps also breaks up into cliques—or as McQueen calls them, affinity groups. Radio people, both men and women, tend to hang out together. Print reporters go out to dinner together, regardless of gender. Television correspondents, because they file their stories twenty-four-hours a day, stick close to their camera crews. The TV technicians, generally blue-collar males, form another subgroup. Fortysomething women reporters, married and with children, may have more in common with married male reporters who are their contemporaries than with younger, single women. The traveling wives and husbands all call home on their cellular phones to check on day-care arrangements and report cards.

In the end, attempts to measure the effect of women journalists on political coverage yields mixed results. The evidence suggests that women have pursued personal materials more than their male counterparts, when they have the opportunity to do so. In 1988, Paul Taylor of the *Washington Post* put the so-called Big A question to Gary Hart, asking the Democratic presidential candidate if he had ever committed adultery. During the 1988 presidential debates, panelist Bernard Shaw of CNN asked Michael Dukakis a question that involved the hypothetical rape of the candidate's wife (the question was tasteless and Dukakis's answer lame). During the 1992 campaign, the *New York Post* teased out a large headline over a slim "item" alleging an affair between George Bush and a former member of his staff. Around the time the story appeared, President Bush coincidentally held a news conference for the White House press pool in Kennebunkport, Maine, to highlight a Middle Eastern initiative. The *Post* story offended several male reporters, who muttered about how they would not ask any such question ("the networks and the mainstream media ought not follow the tabloids through the muck," one male complained). Mary Tillotson of CNN believed otherwise and asked Bush about the report. He denied it, while traditionalists among the press corps rolled their eyeballs. Tillotson defended the propriety of her question: "I'm a reporter assigned to cover the president and I did what I thought was my job," she said. If Tillotson had not asked the question, it turns out, two other reporters would have. Both of them were women.

The effects of new technology on political coverage are easier to measure. Up-to-date campaign reporters, like journalists on any other news assignment, need the basic human-software skills of "getting it and writing it." They still must gather information, ask questions, organize their materials, and present their stories clearly and comprehensively, with balance and fairness. The availability of new hardware including laptops, cellular phones, faxes, and modems—and for television journalists, lightweight cameras, portable uplinks, and computer editing equipment—places greater demands on the journalist-as-processor. For one, everything happens faster. During the Vietnam War, for example, battle film footage traveled by courier from the field to Saigon; there, it was edited, provided with accompanying narrative, then airlifted to Hong Kong or Singapore for another airplane transit to the United States. Two decades later during the Persian Gulf War the American television audience watched in real time while Scud missiles landed in Tel Aviv and reporters described the eerie scene via live satellite transmissions.[4]

The early 1990s were a transitional period, technologically, as the possibilities of the new equipment were explored in uncharted ways. At the most basic level, the new technology began changing the techniques of news gathering. Some of these new uses were ad hoc and ingenious. As the Democratic National Convention approached in July 1992, for example, speculation centered on candidate Clinton's choice for vice president. Late one night, political reporter John King of the Associated Press became annoyed when his pager went off and only the numbers 4-6-7-3 appeared on the LED display. It was 11:30 P.M. King and a hundred other reporters were trolling their sources, attempting to find out the name of Clinton's running mate. King's pager went off two more times, each time displaying the same four digits. What kind of caller cannot leave a proper phone number? King wondered, annoyed at the intrusion. Then it hit him: 4-6-7-3 spells out G-O-R-E on a phone keypad. The AP reporter was being tipped off in code by someone who could not risk an actual conversation. While there is never any substitute for good inside sources in politics, it did not hurt to be equipped with the latest technology either. When King double-checked with Clinton campaign officials before filing a story based on his scoop, he remembered his confidence: "I knew I could say to them, 'Look, I know it's Gore . . . .' That always helps."

As with King, so, too, it was with other members of the traveling corps. The press and the campaign were interconnected not merely for spur-of-the-moment tips but in a systematic way—again, with pervasive effects on the news product. Reporters routinely were reached by both the candidates' fax machines and by desk editors' electronic mail; at the same time, the reporters were able to consult databases and use E-mail from the field. Of the one hundred four political reporters surveyed by the Freedom Forum Media Studies Center in 1992, ninety said they used portable computers during the campaign; one-half said they were equipped with home-office pagers, while nearly that number carried cellular phones.[5] The new technology meant more information was available to campaign reporters using computer modems to download background information; these materials, in turn, helped bring some depth to stories. "We had a lot fewer excuses to be mediocre," King concluded. On the other hand, access to more information often had the unintended consequence of producing more looka-like, soundalike journalism. Database searches and the availability of the daily inside-politics facsimile sheet "Hotline" meant that story narratives were established very fast. The conventional wisdom spread widely and within hours, feeding on the cyber-era equivalent of the old frat-pack journalism. Depending on the theme du jour, the newshounds took up the consensus cry, "Perot not a factor . . . ," or "Perot the spoiler . . . ," or "Clinton's got a lock on the election . . . ," or "The momentum's with Bush . . . ." "Every political reporter in the country had the opportunity to see what every other political reporter did," remembered John Fiedler, senior political correspondent for the *Miami Herald*.

Equally to the point, the new technology began changing the dynamics between field reporter and desk editor, and thus the balance between firsthand observation and home-office "reformulations." The same databases and online services available to the reporters were also available to their editors. Tom Rosenstiel of the *Los Angeles Times*, among others, has pointed out that editors now have an extraordinary array of "public data" streaming into newsrooms: printed transcripts of everything administration officials say, online texts of White House briefings, background papers, etc.[6] He recounted the case of a reporter covering the Clarence Thomas confirmation hearings. The reporter's editors were watching the hearings on television and regularly decided the day's story line. The reporter did not concur with their news judgments; he, after all, was on the scene and had followed the story for months and knew the principals. But the editors could in effect counter, "We were there, too" (and less directly, "You still work for us"). A kind of virtual news developed, composed of the continuous stream of online data and the field reporters' original contributions—all put together by the synthesizer-editors back at the home office.

The journalists covering the interactive campaign could never be too far from television, the stage of contemporary politics, and so their TV sets became essential field equipment, along with their PC's, faxes, and cellular phones. The men and women reporters of the 1990s had scant time for midnight pub-crawling even if they had the inclination. They had to watch the campaign, AKA the national talk show, as it was seen and heard on their hotel-room TV screens: the extensive coverage of speeches, campaign events, and voter call-ins on C-SPAN, the cable channel devoted to politics and public policy; the candidates' appearances on soft-news formats and in the debates; the latest flight of campaign spots; the major congressional hearings. This was, after all, what their readers and their editors were seeing. In a time of electronic populism, the television "reality" *was* the campaign "reality."

With so many real-time events on television, the old-line network news organizations have had to recast their traditional modes of coverage—another systemic response to changing technology and the new campaign reality. The evening news programs have shifted away from spot news to more analytical stories. If the audience has already seen the debate or heard the town meeting, the networks' reasoning goes, then we have to provide the background reporting. In 1992, "American Agenda" on ABC's *World News Tonight, CBS Evening News'* "Reality Check," CNN's "Inside Politics," and NBC News' "Ad Watch" and "Voice of the People" all were attempts to go beyond events to do more contextual journalism. Inevitably, the national talk-show gab became a point of departure for the evening news' own work. Before the 1992 campaign, Bill Wheatley, director of political coverage for NBC, acknowledged, "no one would have imagined the Larry King phenomenon." Post-1992, no one can imagine a campaign without the soft-media formats.

The television people on the bus in the 1960s and 1970s spent their time trying to get close to the candidates. Erik Sorenson, executive producer of the *CBS Evening News* during the 1992 campaign, recalled a conversation he had with a CBS producer who covered the candidates in the old days. Then, "it was a big deal if you could get your camera close to the president or the challenger and get a shot of 'the man in the crowd' . . . you'd call up excited about how really really close you were, overhearing him saying to a child, 'the future is yours'." Post-Vietnam and post-Watergate, both television and the crowd were less enamored with the man in their midst. The candidates understood people's growing anger (or apathy) and relied more on made-for-TV events. By the late 1980s, operatives like Roger Ailes had perfected the art of controlling the campaign message. During the 1988 presidential campaign, acknowledges Steve Friedman, then-executive producer of NBC's *Nightly News,* the only events examined were those that "the campaigns were showing."

That left some news organizations with the novel option of getting off the bus, literally, and trying to provide coverage outside the candidates' daily routine of repetitive speeches and canned events. On *CBS News'* "Reality Check," candidate claims of one kind or another—in a speech or a political commercial—are examined from the consumers' point of view. The distinguishing graphic for each segment is an iconic stamp that looked like the Good Housekeeping Seal of Approval. "Reality Check" identifies a problem, say, loss of jobs to foreign countries, and attempts to explain what the candidates have said or done about it. In Erik Sorenson's words, "we're trying to hold their feet to the fire." In the 1992 campaign and in its planning for 1996, NBC decided that its correspondents should board the campaign planes and busses only intermittently. NBC may not cultivate the White House's traveling staff well enough, but whatever inside sources are lost, the network tries to make up with a fresh perspective and more interactions with the audience-electorate. The pointedly interactive segment "Voice of the People" features correspondent Bob Kur's interviews with voters on the tarmac and at factory gates before the candidate arrives. Instead of riding on the bus and looking at the campaign world from the inside out, journalists like Kur stand outside, next to the voters, and look in.

The voice of the electorate is allowed to speak up in such segments, to a point. The voting public is heard in a less direct way as well. It is a truism of media and politics that both news consumption and voter turnout are related to age: the older the man or woman, the more likely he or she reads a newspaper or magazine, watches TV news—and goes to the polls on election day. Politicians and news organizations alike want to win the voters' approval—for the one, on election day; for the other, in the nightly ratings. But not all members of the audience are equally coveted. Both the parties and the media have targeted a specific demographic segment in the 1990s: younger American men and women who are often aliterate and apolitical. That is, they know how to read but many choose not to; they are eligible to vote but stay at home. The music television channel has helped define this audience and given it a name: the MTV generation.[7]

The influence of MTV on American youth and its politics is widely and enthusiastically accepted, although relatively few critics have actually bothered to examine MTV's supposed "counterculture effect." The few skeptics who have cast a cold eye on cool MTV quickly spotted its capitalist soul underneath the lyrics about racist cops and the plight of the rain forest. Ostensibly scorning "American materialism" and the corrupt values of bourgeois parents, MTV actually is one long commercial for consumerism. The core music-video programming sells CDs and the avowedly commercial advertising spots between the videos push soft drinks, jeans, and other gear.[8] But the actual content of MTV did not matter. Some White House operatives and most mainstream media *act* as if MTV is as important in its way as are the gender shifts and the arrival of new technology.

Thus, during the 1992 presidential race and since, the traditionalist *CBS Evening News* has adopted an MTV look from time to time. During the Bush campaign, one CBS newscast opened with a Polydor/PLG Records video; instead of rap music, however, a voiceover of Bush repeating the phrase "read my lips" was laid down, to synthesizer accompaniment. "Yes, stylistically we did some slick stuff," said Susan Zirinsky, the director of CBS News' political coverage at the time. "We're a society that watches MTV, and we tried to reach those people." The same month, the "Brokaw Report" on NBC featured interview segments with Clinton and Bush; each man was surrounded by a screen full of MTV-like slogans—"White House," "health," "gay rights," and "conservative." On ABC's *World News Tonight,* in October 1992, Peter Jennings gave a straightforward report on the president's veto of the cable-industry regulation bill and then offered a kind of music video: a rapid-fire sequence of Bush at campaign stops across the country, with the audio repeating the president's words, "gridlock Congress, gridlock Congress," as the camera cut from one speech to another. Even casual viewers of the news programs produced by the Fox network have picked up on the odd camera angles, quick jump-cuts, day-glo graphics and computer-produced images intended to entice an audience of reputedly jaded young adults.

By the presidential election of 2000, a new campaign journalism may emerge. The same satellite technology that speeds the transmission of messages may also alter the content of that information stream. In 1992, when the first stories alleging Bill Clinton's involvement with Gennifer Flowers appeared, newspapers such as the *Miami Herald,* the *New York Times,* the *Los Angeles Times,* and the *Washington Post,* as well as the major networks and the *MacNeil-Lehrer NewsHour,* initially ignored Flowers and her tapes or gave them extremely modest attention. Flowers's sponsors, the supermarket tabloid, *Star,* then staged a news conference in New York. The conference was carried on the network feed—the not-for-broadcast transmissions from the network headquarters of ABC, CBS, and NBC to local-affiliate stations and to network bureaus. Such raw materials—an apt designation in this case—are then edited for possible later use as excerpts on the evening newscasts. But when the Flowers's news conference was announced, the affiliates demanded the feed for full, real-time use. They received the news conference live and unedited and put it on their local news shows. The local stations' capability to download the feed from satellites pushed the Flowers story ahead. Without that pressure, Flowers might have been no more than a tough question in some parlor game of trivia. As it is, she has secured her own pedicured footnote in history, along with Paula Jones.

The fact that the raw feed itself can become part of the national political narrative raises some intriguing interactive possibilities for campaign 1996, campaign 2000, and on and on. A documentary about the 1992 campaign called simply "Feed" appeared in art-house theaters around the country just before election time. The impish producers of "Feed," acting without anyone's permission, and using their own equipment, simply recorded the networks' satellite transmissions. Then they assembled the tapes of candidates, anchors, and reporters waiting for events to begin. "Feed" captured the boredom, artifice, and at times, sappiness of the process: the unguarded moments that not even C-SPAN shows. In a few years, ordinary citizens will have access to the low-cost technology used to pull down the raw footage of the "feed" from satellites and compile their own campaign record. They will be able to bypass everyone: old and new media, reporters and editors, traditional observers and cybersynthesizers. Electronic populism cannot get any more populist than that.

Pixilated: Governing by Teledemocracy

It seemed like old times for Bill Clinton . . . tossing the conversation ball around with Don Imus during morning drive time on New York radio station WFAN . . . trolling for support in a Cleveland mall . . . taking questions from suburban Chicago high school students . . . then heading west, to parachute down on San Diego for a television call-in show. Meanwhile, Hillary Rodham Clinton held a satellite town meeting on health care for a West Virginia statewide television network.

The only problem was, old times—campaign '92—were over. Candidate Clinton became president, and his wife the first lady. Yet there they were trying to run the country as if still in campaign mode, using the pop media, drop-in TV, and interactive technology. The obituaries for his "failed presidency" seemed a bit premature: President Clinton was able to accomplish a part of his legislative agenda. He also could count on a modest reservoir of public goodwill; Americans, by and large, want their president to succeed. Most citizens understand that, as Lyndon Johnson was credited with saying, "I'm the only president you've got." But one major Clintonian brainstorm quickly shortcircuited. No matter how promising the techniques of electronic democracy, not even the most telegenic president can govern from the road. Patriotism has its limits.

The Clintonites tried to "reinvent government" during the first three years of their administration. Clinton's media specialists still insisted that, in their standard formulation, "the president likes to talk to people, not through people." Translating from New Age-speak, the Clinton White House preferred to go around the traditional institutions of the Congress, the bureaucracy, and the Washington press corps to reach the citizen-voters directly—unfiltered, unanalyzed, and unchallenged. Inconveniently, though, when he was elected president, Clinton became a major part of the old institutionalized system. That made it logically difficult, although emotionally satisfying, to campaign against "Washington"—the Washington punditocracy and the White House press corps can be an arrogant, blinkered lot, given to singing from the same conventional sheet music. Worse, for the success of Clinton's own programs, the voting classes still get most of their news and commentary from what the New Agers call, rather condescendingly, the "traditional press." And so, President Clinton's failure to win over those Washington monuments of power hobbled his effectiveness and hurt his legislative program.

This was never more evident than in the winter of 1993–94, when an odd collection of stories about Bill and Hillary Clinton's underreported income, cattle-futures' trading, and soured land deals became known by the catchall headline, "Whitewater." (Two decades before, "Watergate" became the portmanteau word for a much more serious collection of acts ranging from improprieties to actual felonies committed by the White House staff and its operatives.) The earliest reporting of the stories that metastasized into Whitewater appeared in the mainstream *New York Times*. Most of the subsequent materials came from right-wing political action groups and "congressional sources"—read, gleeful Republicans—and the investigative work of the *Times*, the *Wall Street Journal*, and the

Washington Post. Similarly, the most damning materials about Clinton's private sexual escapades came from the traditionalist *Los Angeles Times;* some smarmier work was also done by the freelance writer David Brock, whose writing appeared in the Washington-based conservative monthly, the *American Spectator.* The Washington bureau of CNN picked up and amplified aspects of the story, in particular the allegations of four Arkansas state troopers that they had stood guard or otherwise helped provide cover for Clinton during a string of sexual liaisons when he was governor in the 1980s.[1]

The president's job ratings declined in the weeks and months after these stories appeared. For example, a *Washington Post*-ABC News poll queried a random sample of the electorate about its attitudes toward the president once in January 1993, at the time of the inauguration, and again in March 1994, during a flood of Whitewater allegations. Asked "are you satisfied that Bill Clinton has the honesty and integrity to serve effectively as President?" 74 percent of the inauguration sample answered, "yes." Fourteen months later, during the Whitewater high tide, the "yes" answers had dropped to 63 percent. The "integrity index" then leveled off around that number. But by mid-1994, *Washington Post*-ABC polling showed Clinton losing public support over his perceived foreign policy "failures" in Bosnia, Haiti, and Rwanda. At one point, the president's job ratings dropped perilously close to 43 percent, the percentage of the vote he received in 1992.[2]

The information that precipitated the drop in the president's approval ratings came from stories that the citizenry read in its old-media morning newspapers or saw on the traditionalist evening news shows. Larry King, MTV, and the new media provided limited facts about the making of foreign policy or the General Agreement on Tariffs and Trade (GATT) and the G-7 meetings. For that matter, the soft-news formats carried little hard data on the Madison Savings and Loan deal, the Clintons' 1979 joint tax returns, and the troopers' tales of sexual athleticism. Just as the pop media had little to do with shaping the public's attitudes toward Clinton on these matters, the mainstream press's influence was somewhat limited as well. The public did not buy the overly glib attempt to suggest Whitewater was a scandal of the dimensions of Watergate, and that the Clintons' wheelings and dealings in Little Rock were somehow akin to the Nixon-era crimes involving the White House and federal agencies. A majority of those sampled still wanted to believe in the integrity of the president. The constant rush of Whitewater did not erode this base, suggesting that on certain matters the public makes its decisions independent of *both* hard- and soft-news sources. Or, alternatively, some public opinions are not easily changed: they have hardened over time, like drying concrete.

Further, the subjects of their opinions may not be the kind that stirs passions. Many Americans' interests in foreign policy or national politics may be somewhat akin to their interests in foreign or national weather. We take note, intellectually, in our newspapers or on morning television, that snow storms are predicted in Wyoming. Unless we live in Laramie, that information has little impact on our daily lives. If the snow were piling up outside our own door, that would be something else. This is not to say people are selfish; they are self-interested. Personal absorption does not rule out empathy for others; when an earthquake strikes Los Angeles, we phone relatives to ask how they are.

The fact that many people live lives focused around their houses rather than around the White House upset some of the more unforgiving partisans. Instead of praising the citizenry for maturity and the ability to take things in stride, the anti-Clinton forces blamed the messengers. The usual (conservative) suspects sent up the usual cry of (liberal) press favoritism. R. Emmitt Tyrell, Jr., editor of the *American Spectator,* announced that the Clintonites had been "surprisingly effective in muzzling the Washington press corps." Although it was true that the sex story never developed in a sustained way—even the attempt to call it "Troopergate" seemed forced—Tyrell and the bloviating Sunday morning commentators missed what was really going on. Clinton dodged that particular bullet, not because of a supine press, or because of the outrageousness of tales. The *American Spectator* article, the *Los Angeles Times* story, and the CNN report about then-Governor Clinton's womanizing all came out around the Christmas-New Year's rush; Americans were, once again, otherwise engaged with their own private affairs. Moreover, the stories were the equivalent of snow in Wyoming: old news. The troopers' tales recycled what a lot of the public already assumed, or believed.

The same pattern repeated itself when a former Arkansas state employee named Paula Corbin Jones came forward a few months later to allege an improper sexual advance by Clinton during his last year as governor of Arkansas (roughly the same period covered in the *Los Angeles Times-American Spectator*-CNN stories). The Jones account registered high on the prurience scale; she claimed that the governor had propositioned her in a Little Rock hotel room (she said he asked for oral sex after the briefest of small talk). The circumstances of her disclosure added to the raunch level: Jones went public with her story almost three years after the alleged episode, and she did so at a Washington news conference held during a meeting of a conservative political action committee. Her first set of lawyers tried to broker a cash settlement with the White House, and one of Jones's sisters told reporters that "[Paula] smelled money" whatever way the deal swung. That is, she would get a payday, either in the form of hush payments from Clinton or from the sale of her exclusive story to tabloid TV shows and other cash-for-trash outlets. Once again, the mainstream press dithered about how far it should be pulled along by the ruder media. In the main, the major news outlets waited for the fig leaf of a hard-news event to use as cover for its attention. When Jones filed a lawsuit alleging emotional distress and violation of her civil rights—the statute of limitations had run out for a sexual harassment suit—the mainstream decided that it now had its needed news peg and legitimate justification for running Jones's account of how she came to be in the hotel room and what supposedly happened. *People* magazine, a reliable barometer of popular taste, accorded Jones her fifteen minutes of celebrity, putting her on its May 23, 1994, cover. In 1974, when *People* began publication, critics dismissed it as no more than a fast read while spending a few minutes under the hair dryer. By the 1990s, that early put-down had been turned into a boast by the magazine's sales staff, who claimed that 3 million demographically desirable young women passed *People* around in beauty shops each week.

The beauty-parlor talk about Clinton and Jones was more bemused than bitter during the spring of 1994. It was a discussion on the level of conversation about Wyoming weather . . . something happening somewhere else. People who read *People* were smart enough to recognize that anyone can file a lawsuit and entice old and new media to cover it, but that neither the suit nor the publicity meant the allegations were true. More: it was a *familiar* weather report. The audience had been presented with candidate Clinton's confession of an "imperfect" marriage at the time of the New Hampshire primary. Questions about his honesty and integrity also had been aired during the fall campaign. "We had that referendum in 1992," a veteran Republican strategist told us, glumly but realistically. "The voters had a choice between skirt-chasing, pot-smoking, draft-dodging Bill Clinton and George Bush. And you know how they voted."

Clinton's media skills helped him on call-in shows and at town meetings. It was a stroke of genius to book Bill and Hillary Clinton as a team on the CBS magazine show *60 Minutes,* so that he could talk about the "imperfections in his marriage" while she listened alongside him, standing by her man even as he implicitly confessed past infidelities. But the Clinton White House hardly invented electronic populism. Ronald Reagan used his video talents to complain about "gummint" and earned the designation "communicator in chief." His successor, George Bush, built the first satellite-uplink studio in the Old Executive Office Building next to the White House. Unfortunately for the Republicans, Bush was never very good as a television salesman, even when fielding the softball questions pitched via satellite from local-station interviewers and anchors. In the 1992 campaign, Clinton was slower to use the new media than other candidates, most prominently, H. Ross Perot (the Larry King candidate, announcing his availability on the CNN call-in show and campaigning with TV infomercials and appearances on soft-news programs). Print—a news story on the front page of the *New York Times*—does not matter any more, Perot told the *Times*. "It just blows away."

The Clinton image team more modestly used the new media as a "parallel track" alongside the traditional press. The campaign's media consultants Mandy Grunwald and Frank Greer, architects of the strategy, advised Clinton that "moments of passion, personal reflection and humor (available in these popular cultural programs) do more for us than any six-second soundbite on the network news . . ." It became part of the Clinton canon that his use of town meetings, televised within New Hampshire, helped shore up support after the Gennifer Flowers story appeared in the down-market checkout-counter weekly, the *Enquirer* (the *60 Minutes* appearance was aimed at a national audience). Similarly, candidate Clinton's appearances on Don Imus, Phil Donahue, et al. helped him with the New York primary after his mediocre showing in Connecticut. This was taken as evidence that the new media can be used to overcome bad press in the old media (that is, speaking *to* people rather than *through* people). Inevitably, then, when President Clinton started to sink in the polls, he went back on the road. In these new presentations—campaign '93, campaign '94, campaign '95—the interactions with Imus, the mall trolling, the call-in shows, and the MTV town meetings were part of a strategy to build a teledemocracy base in the country in order to fight the insiders back in Washington. "The way they saw it," Andrea Mitchell of NBC News told us, "the new media have always worked for them."

But in his first three years as president, Clinton never again enjoyed quite the successes he had in 1992. Month after month, the media advisers' parallel track plan kept leaving the rails. Early in 1993, the Hollywood producer Harry Thomason received a coveted White House access pass and moved into a temporary office in the Executive Office Building, located not far from its satellite TV studio. Thomason and his wife and co-producer Linda Bloodworth-Thomason were longtime friends of the Clintons. The Thomasons' television credits included "Designing Women" and "Evening Shade," as well as "The Man from Hope," the affecting film biography of Clinton shown during prime time at the Democratic National Convention in 1992. They also produced the presidential inaugural ceremonies in January 1993. But the Thomasons never fit into the Washington culture—the couple's obvious contempt for the resident journalists did not help. Their status as a Hollywood power couple suffered further through a series of small political mishaps that loomed large only in Washington; when Linda Bloodworth-Thomason was interviewed on a morning talk program, she came across as snappish and arrogant. Both husband and wife were back in California before the tulips came out on the White House lawn. Fortunately for their image and egos they were not around to take the heat when two of the administration's most cherished plans for "grassroots" initiatives withered and died. One was a national campaign to promote health-care reforms; the other was a plan for "reinventing government."

The health-care campaign began boldly under the sponsorship of the Democratic National Committee; Richard F. Celeste, a former governor of Ohio, was appointed campaign manager. As initially envisioned, the DNC and Celeste were going to build popular demand for change through a series of new-media measures including: a national petition drive; up to sixty meetings scheduled on a single Town Meeting Day; Perot-style infomercials on television; the appearance of celebrity endorsers to take questions on call-in programs; interactive satellite links joining citizens and government officials; and door-to-door visits by volunteers who were supposed to explain, in Avon Lady fashion, the health-care proposals. "They wanted to re-invent *everything,* including the political process," remembered *USA Today* reporter Judy Keen.[3]

The publicity campaign actually began on a Tuesday in September 1993, the day before the president presented his health-care proposals to the Congress. The first couple had a few newfound friends over for lunch. The White House guest list included the establishment journalists David Broder, R. W. Apple, Jr., Jack Nelson, Gerald Seib, Jack Germond, and Michael Kinsley. The next day, Apple, Seib, Nelson, and Broder found some upbeat news to write about the Clintons and their plan for the readers of, respectively, the *New York Times,* the *Wall Street Journal,* the *Los Angeles Times,* and the *Washington Post.* Nelson and Seib, for example, praised Clinton for his "willingness to negotiate" on details of the health-care plan—the spin the Clintons were serving at lunch along with the salmon fumé. The *New York Times'* Apple, in particular, proved the value of White House bread cast upon the media waters. He likened Clinton's plan to the reforms of Franklin Roosevelt and Lyndon Johnson, grandly discerning the zeitgeist of the administration during his noontime stopover: "The social engineer's optimism that often gripped the White House as Lyndon B. Johnson pushed through the Great Society gripped it today." For a dessert of sorts, Apple evoked the Kennedy Camelot years; the Clintons, he wrote, were positively "radiating enthusiasm."

The same week as the luncheon for the mandarins of print, the Clintons invited some other more déclassé guests. First, the president briefed à group of 200 radio talk-show hosts on his health-care goals. Two days later, the administration invited fifty of the talk-show hosts to originate their morning shows from the front lawn of the White House. The then White House Chief of Staff Thomas McLarty III, Communications Director Mark Gearan, and Media Affairs Director Jeff Eller all were made available to offer "actualities"—radio interviews—on the topic of health care. "A good move for the White House and for the product," recalled one of the invitees, Judy Jarvis of radio station WPOP in Hartford, Connecticut. "Talk radio is probably more connected with what people are really thinking than any other medium." But the thoughts of "the people" and of the radio hosts were not always focused on insurance deductibles and managed care. Barbara Carlson of station KSTP in Minneapolis proffered an on-air invitation to Mark Gearan to share a hot tub with her, while senior Clinton adviser George Stephanopoulos, struggling to be polite, responded to questions about his status as a sex symbol.

The administration's efforts to get public opinion behind health care turned on using both the traditional press and the pop media. The Clintonites tried to overcome their visceral distrust of the establishment press. They began to recognize the power of incumbency and its uses. The White House remains, as Gerald Seib told us, "a powerful message machine: they have the ability to influence what people in the press say, just by letting them in the doors." If you invite the big-time journalists, they will come. Further, these newspaper columnists and magazine writers are read by the television producers and talk-show hosts and influence their decisions about what is news. Print, Jack Nelson suggested, "sets the tone for the way stories are treated," and this tone is reflected by other nonprint outlets.

Part of Nelson's theory was confirmed when we tracked the way the health-care story was covered by old and new media over the last half of 1993 and the first half of 1994.[4] In a way, so too was part of Judy Jarvis's theory. Each had an insight into the communications model that best explains what happened, or rather, what was supposed to happen. The plan for the health-care initiative involved using the popular media to help sell health care as "product": the news broadcasts, talk shows, and town meetings were supposed to let consumers know that it was ready for the retail shelves. At the same time, the administration was going to use the punditocracy to explain the fine print of the plan—the label—to this same public. As marketing specialists might put it, the talk shows and pop formats would give the product mass brand-name recognition, while traditional print explained to the skeptical consumer how to use the product.

So much for the plan. In fact, nothing much happened between the product introduction in September 1993 and the next major media effort in January 1994, when the president extolled health care before a national television audience in his State of the Union address. That was "a long hiatus," Harold Ickes, the White House deputy chief of staff, acknowledged to the *Washington Post* in a March 1994 interview. In retrospect, it was easy to point an accusing finger at the bad "sales people" in the White House: the senior aide who came across as arrogant in his dealings with the Congress; the press officer who occupied himself less with his health-care selling job and more with angling for another, higher position; or the third younger aide who, according to Julie Kosterlitz of the *National Journal*, "spent an inordinate amount of time fiddling with the design of the 'health security card'" that the president eventually used as a prop during his State of the Union speech. Worse, while the White House fiddled, the Clinton health-care opposition—specifically, the insurance company trade group, the Health Insurance Association of America—was burning up home screens with its "Harry and Louise" television advertisements. An affluent-looking fortyish couple, "Harry and Louise" sat in their picture-perfect den, earnestly poring over the pages of Clinton's health plan, furrowing their brows and noting troublesome "hidden costs" and the loss of "provider choice"—all in thirty seconds.

While TV viewers were being asked to empathize with the worried yuppies "Harry and Louise," the Democratic National Committee did little except talk about its grassroots plans. The DNC campaign had a semi-catchy slogan, "Health Care That's Always There," and it had a chairman, Richard F. Celeste, who was neither a major national political presence nor a health-care expert. After hiring two dozen field organizers and spending $2 million, the grassroots plan was abandoned in the spring of 1994. In place of bold, new interactive ventures, the DNC decided to raise funds for traditional paid advertising—thirty-second spots—on mainstream television. "The expectation curve has been an up-and-down one," Celeste told the *Washington Post* blandly. A month later, he was down and out, packing his files to return to his consulting business back home in Columbus.

The White House's courtship of both the old and the new media made use of that time-honored technique of presidential news management, the promise of insider interviews and information. The Clintons' lunch meeting with select print journalists, for instance, was followed by more such "exclusive" interviews with the first couple. Hillary Rodham Clinton appeared with Tom Brokaw later that same day on the *NBC Nightly News;* the next day, she talked with Dan Rather on the *CBS Evening News.* Both anchors accepted Hillary Clinton's assurance that the new health-care plan would reduce rather than increase the bureaucratic apparatus. Rather complimented Mrs. Clinton on her understanding of the complexities of the health-care plan. "I don't know anybody who isn't impressed by your grasp of the details of this plan," he said. (Considering that she devoted six months to developing the plan, the more surprising news would have been that she appeared *un*knowledgeable.)

The White House sales job for its Reinventing Government (ReGo) plan to change how government works also tried to use traditional press and pop media to frame the political debate. Vice

President Al Gore, the plan's chief salesman, was made available for press opportunities. Pop TV show appearances were designed to alert viewers to the brand name, while print journalists were given one-on-one access to Gore. Correspondent Gwen Ifill's "exclusive" story with Gore for the *New York Times* accompanied the vice president, "microphone in hand, sweat soaking his blue shirt," on a stroll through the Pentagon courtyard. Gore was depicted on a fact-finding mission, meeting with federal employees to learn firsthand the banalities of the federal bureaucracy. "If ever a temperament was matched to a task, this is it," Ifill wrote. When *Time* magazine's Margaret Carlson arrived for her interview on ReGo, she found the vice president "standing tall," the administration's "reformer, legislative arm twister and adviser in chief."

The promise of access was enough for the traditionalists of the print press; but the pop formats needed more showy business and more visuals. The White House imagemakers equipped the vice president with the necessary props and booked him on CBS's *Late Show with David Letterman.* (A year later, Senator Bob Dole, trying to advance *his* presidential candidacy, went on Letterman and became in essence his own show-biz prop—genial, joking Bobster instead of dour Kansas conservative.) Some 19 million viewers watched as Gore and Letterman donned safety goggles and the vice president smashed an ashtray with a hammer—a demonstration of the craziness of federal regulations. "They actually specify the exact way people have to break this in order to test it," Gore explained, trying to give a "practical" example of what ReGo was intended to change. After the Letterman appearance, Gore completed a three-day tour of pop outlets, including *Larry King Live,* the *Today Show,* and the *"Donahue"* show. Gore came on the *Donahue* set carrying a bottle of government-issue floor wax and a three-quarter-inch-thick stack of regulations dictating federal use of the wax. He said he wanted to show a "stupid government trick."

The White House got an extra bounce from the Gore show. The *New York Times, USA Today,* and the *Los Angeles Times,* among others, ran articles about the vice president's guest appearance on Letterman. Marketplace identification for ReGo was achieved. But could the Clintonites close the sale? When Gore said his goodbyes on Letterman, the host wished him well, and used signature Lettermanesque irony to put distance between himself and his guest. "Good luck with that government thing," Letterman said. By the summer of 1994, the administration had also distanced itself from ReGo, and the plan vanished from public consciousness. The Clintons' sales energies had shifted back to promoting their health-care plan, a product desperately needing help.

Beliefs in the power of the visual arts die hard. When public support for the Clinton version of health-care reform steadily dropped in the months after its introduction, both supporters and enemies of the administration's plan talked of the marketing triumphs and failures: the slickness of "Harry and Louise," the bumbling DNC and White House campaign, etc. The Clintonites resisted seeing their problem as one of product rather than of sales effort; they continued to maintain faith in the talisman of new media formats. In April 1994, while marking time until the release of the independent prosecutor's report on Whitewater, Clinton ventured out again to MTV for a town meeting. On a cloudy spring day, he went to the Kalorama film studios in northwest Washington to record a ninety-minute tape. The high school and college student audience was selected by MTV as was the theme, "Enough is Enough"—meaning it is time to stop the violence plaguing America. One of the MTV co-hosts was Tabitha Soren, reprising the role she had played in Clinton's first appearance on the twenty-four-hour music video channel during the 1992 campaign. The White House staff saw in the MTV show a chance to build support for the administration's crime bill, then under consideration in the Congress, as well as an opportunity to buff Clinton's image as a leader in touch with America's youth. The public relations plan derailed toward the end of the question-and-answer segment, when seventeen-year-old Laetitia Thompson, wearing ragged jeans and a snug black top, was handed the microphone. She asked if the president wore boxer shorts or briefs. He revealed that he was a briefs man. Their exchange became the storyline of the news accounts of Clinton's MTV appearance the next day, all but crowding out his antiviolence message. The president himself had shaken his head at his teenage questioner; "I can't believe she did that," he said on camera. Live and learn. The *Washington Post* produced a *second* story on the president's choice of underwear a day later; it was full of dumb puns—"President Loses Some Support"—and sniggering innuendo: a continuing White House PR disaster.

"They thought they could accomplish anything through public relations—print a brochure, go on the tube, do a town meeting," said Andrea Mitchell, NBC's White House correspondent (and, in the Clintonites' eyes, a representative of the old ways). "They felt that they didn't have to deal with Senator Dole or the Washington press corps." Apparently everyone but the Clinton team grasped the principle that, when it came to getting legislation through the Congress, the Bob Doles—and the Andrea Mitchells—were more important than Larry King, Tabitha Soren, and the rest of the new media. The Congress, the Washington press, and the other players inside the system, for all their inbred elitism, still supplied the analytical context and the critical judgment necessary for good policymaking. It was hard to live with the Washington establishment; but no president could live *without* it. After the Republicans won control of both chambers of the Congress in the November 1994, elections, Clinton had to deal with the ultimate established power: a united opposition led in the House by Speaker Newt Gingrich and backed by an organized, ideologically pure voting majority.

The fate of Clinton's health-care legislation in the last days of the 103rd Congress, in the fall of 1994, demonstrated not only the power of the Newt Gingriches and the Andrea Mitchells, but also the limits of presidential power in the new interactive culture. For a half century now, presidents have had to contend with an increasingly adversarial press—for good reason: half-truths, dissembling, and evasion have become part of the American way of political life, as natural as breathing. By the 1990s, the White House was under twenty-four-hour scrutiny by journalists (capable, in truth, of their own little mendacities). Clinton's struggle to govern was also hampered by his own (and his staff's) disorganized, frenetic, ahistorical style. They were easy snacks for the press watchdogs, because the pack in some ways was like the Clintonites: it had an excess of power and a dearth of experience. Over the last three decades, journalists have been bred to value "vigilance" (at least in its outward form). And so, the Washington press pack barked incessantly, often mistaking shadows for matters of substance.

When the corpse of health-care reform was found sprawled on Capitol Hill after Congress scattered for the November elections, the pack was as much in the dark as the assorted friends of the deceased. Health-care legislation was dead for 1994. Whodunit? Hillary Rodham Clinton, a person closely identified with the victim, blamed *unnatural* causes: shadowy special interests who used paid media to "misrepresent" the administration's proposals (the "Harry and Louise" spots as blunt instrument). The *New York Times* turned to Agatha Christie's *Murder on the Orient Express*. According to political writer Robin Toner, several suspects "had their hands on the knife at one time or another"—the overbeaverish wonks of the Clinton administration; divided congressional Democrats; natural-born killer-partisans of the Republican leadership; the cold-eyed capos of the health-insurance industry; and its accomplices from other interest groups. Other obituaries stressed the part played by the media themselves. In a PBS special, "The Great Health Care Debate," presented after the reform measures died in October, host-commentator Bill Moyers pointed accusingly at the talk-show culture. Moyers described how—recovering from major heart surgery and spending his summer listening to hours and hours of radio—he was dismayed to hear that "almost every talk radio host was 'anti-' the Clinton proposals." Political scientist Thomas Patterson of Syracuse University pointed his finger at the mainstream watchdogs. According to Patterson, the modern, complete Washington reporter *aspires* to being "anti-": such journalism instinctively "magnifies the bad and underplays the good" that politicians do.

The idea of snarling, judgmental—and, ultimately, unreliable—newshounds has a certain instant appeal in the search for Washington villainy. In fact, the role of talk-show-culture and Washington journalists in the Clinton White House's apparent inability to govern, as illustrated by the demise of health care in 1994, was more ambiguous than the conventional criticism suggests. It was also more worrisome, not just for the fate of health-care reform but also for the future of all presidential communications.

Both the talk shows and the television ads were (mildly) amusing sideshows during the health-care story of 1993 and 1994. In the midst of the most intense attention to health care, only one in seven Americans could recall ever hearing of the angst-ridden yuppies, "Harry and Louise." But then, the insurance companies' ads were not intended to reach the mass TV audience. "Harry and Louise" were *narrowcast* to produce stories and commentary seen by a Washington policy audience. The ads signaled, in case key members of Congress were not getting the message, that the health-care industry intended to spend big money to defeat plans it did not like. The Clinton administration health-care proposals were not defeated "because of" the talk shows or the TV ads. The real killing ground was the more familiar one of classic Washington political transactions.

Most Americans received most of their information about health care from their newspapers, news magazines, and TV network newscasts. These channels of information all rely on journalism's traditional narrative mode, and that proved enough to speed the demise of reform. Once a story achieves a critical mass of attention—whether in Congress, Haiti, or at a Los Angeles murder trial—coverage follows two predictable patterns. First, "developments" get regular attention even when there is no real news ("This is John Cochran on Capitol Hill, where the noise level over health care is rising . . ."). Second, stories are fitted into a political campaign narrative (charge-rebuttal, attack-counterattack, who's winning and who's losing in the metaphorical "horse race"). In *USA Today,* for example, forty-one articles about health care appeared during a two-month period in early 1994. One dealt primarily with cost; another offered a good explanatory guide and twenty-nine were principally about health care "battles," "challenges," and who was for or against the plan (sample headlines: "CEOs Back Clinton Rival Health Plan," and "Clinton on the Attack in Health Care Debate"). Similarly, in a sampling of thirty-five articles that appeared in *Time* and *Newsweek* during 1993, ten were concerned with Clinton's approval ratings and how the fate of health care would "make or break" his administration.

Could the Clintonites have avoided this media frame for health care, or blunted its effects? Yes, but only to a limited extent. The buck *starts* here, in the White House. That is, the administration made some fateful decisions at the outset in the choice of the product it decided to sell. The reform plan, for example, rejected a single-payer scheme, featuring government as the national insurer. Single-payer had been tested and proved workable in Canada, Germany, France, and other countries; but it was vulnerable to easy, albeit false, caricature as "socialized medicine." Given the congressional Republican leadership's obstructionist stance, single-payer was understandably mischaracterized from the outset: Newt Gingrich wanted to be the House Speaker for a conservative majority, not a bipartisan player on a statist team attempting to pass single-payer legislation. And, given the press's sporting tastes, it is certain that the ensuing high-visibility, mediagenic "fight" would attract the journalists' attention faster than off-camera digging in

Ottawa, Paris, or Bonn. Consequently, the facts about true costs, choice, and controls never really came out.

Perhaps health care was such a vast, complex, confusing subject that the journalists—short of time, patience, knowledge—took the quickest way out by doing political process stories. "Horse race," after all, is easier to report and analyze than health-maintenance organizations (HMOs) and purchasing co-ops. The attack-talk culture that so disturbed Moyers, by contrast, has no excuse: it makes no pretense at either unblinkered reporting or honest analysis. Interest-group ads are, by definition, one sided; so too, the talk-show hosts, whose idea of "research" is to read the AP wire before airtime. Their minds are made up; these races are fixed.

There are indeed "losers" when the public dialogue is set by the new yakkers' culture. While an already fearful electorate was pumped up with constant, dire bulletins about what was happening politically in the health-care "battle," it got relatively little information about the actual content of the various reform proposals. After all the insider ads and campaign-style coverage of who's up and who's down, most Americans were still clueless about the true costs and benefits of universal coverage. To this day, for example, only one in five citizens can define for pollsters the term "managed care" (we wonder how many journalists and talk-show hosts are similarly dazed and confused). Like everyone else, we were transfixed by the race; we mourned—or cheered—the result. In all the excitement, though, it was easy to lose sight of what the process was all about.

The old media habit of choosing conflict over context, and the new media addiction to monomaniacal attack, may make it all but impossible for even the best organized, most adept White House to govern effectively. For the sake of argument, assume the Clintonite workforce had the skills and efficiencies of, say, the Lexus assembly line. That may not be enough to overcome consumer resistance. The twenty-four-hour talk racket makes an already edgy electorate more jumpy. So does the political fight model of coverage, stoking paranoidal fantasies of dark deals going down and feeding suspicions of business as usual. As a consequence, a straggling line of one-term presidents may stretch into the millennium: first, Bush, now Clinton, next, his successor.

The series of setbacks on health care, ReGo, et al. dimmed but did not extinguish the White House's zeal for teledemocracy. Clinton and Gore used their authority to keep boosting the information superhighway. They became proponents of a fiber-optics data transmission system that offered such services as teleconferencing, interactive multimedia education, home shopping, and on-demand news and information searches. These would be "the pixels in a rapidly expanding picture," as the computer enthusiasts put it. In this millennial view, more and more human interactions will take place electronically, in cyberspace. Like the Perot candidacy, we will all exist "in the air." The Clinton White House began to use online computer services and E-mail to communicate with the electorate. On CompuServe, the president could be addressed electronically by typing 75300,3115. His America Online address was ClintonPZ. On MCI, a simple "White House" began communications. The computer modem did the rest. Electronically challenged citizens who owned only a touchtone phone could call the "White House comments line" and use the keypad to punch in responses. The White House also uploaded information. Typing the command GO WHITEHOUSE on CompuServe produced the message "Welcome to the White House Forum." The retrieval menu included presidential speeches as well as texts of background briefings.

Again, the suspicious watchdogs of the press detected presidential avoidance of the old media in order to reach The People. The Clintonites presented it differently, as a means of furthering democratic communications. Jonathan "Jock" Gill, a former software development specialist, worked in the White House communications office, upgrading the cyberspace facilities. According to

Gill, in the past few years business cards routinely began including fax numbers along with phone numbers; similarly, in a few years from now, "everybody's cards will carry their E-mail numbers." White House reporters will use their numbers to address the president's computer, if not the man himself. Presumably, the virtual answers to their virtual questions will somehow approximate the reality of a traditional news conference.

Hillary Rodham Clinton Meets the Press: An East-Wing Case Study

The president and his staff operate out of the Oval Office and the White House West Wing. In the East Wing are the offices of the first lady (in the now-quaint usage of Washington protocol and the Washington press corps). The manner in which Hillary Rodham Clinton has been covered during the first years of the Clinton administration deserves separate examination. The Hillary story is an example of how media narratives are shaped by factors independent of both the content of the message being transmitted and the particular medium of transmission. Among the most important of these factors is the storytellers' desire to engage their target audience. The consumer really is given what he or she wants.

Hillary Clinton was sought after by both the mainstream press and the new media from the time she began appearing at campaign stops. She received greater attention than the wife of any candidate in memory (Jacqueline Kennedy did not emerge as a media icon until after the election of her husband).[5] In age, status, and occupation, Hillary Clinton neatly matched the interests of the target audiences the popular media were trying to reach. On the conservative talk shows and in special-interest magazines like the right-wing *American Spectator,* the audience's interests naturally worked against her. Millions of talk-radio listeners were not just conservatives opposed to the Clintons' "liberalism"; they were young, white-collar males wary of strong-looking women. "Power women," like Hillary Clinton were presented in a way that stirred the target audience's worst fears of uppity, ambitious, pushy, castrating women who wanted their jobs or were quick to file sexual harassment suits for the mildest of office banter. In a dreaded word, she was a "feminist." Rush Limbaugh, in fact, popularized the term, "femi-nazis," while the *American Spectator* depicted Hillary Clinton on its cover in a witch's hat, riding a broom. The pop media's Hillary-haters wanted it both ways, implying that she was a closet lesbian and at the same time insinuating that she had a long-term affair with Vincent Foster, the Little Rock lawyer who joined the White House staff and later committed suicide. To square the circle of innuendo, cable television's Reverend Jerry Falwell announced his suspicions that Foster had been murdered (despite an FBI investigation concluding that Foster took his own life).

The coverage in the mainstream newspapers, magazines, and television networks also played to their core audiences, albeit constituencies that were broader and less pinched than the talk-show boys. The mainstream—and its advertisers—wanted readers and viewers who were, demographically speaking, like Bill and Hillary Clinton, that is, in their peak consumer years. The editors of the *Ladies Home Journal* understood the convergence of first lady and desired advertising demographic when they asked on the cover of their April 1993 issue: "Hillary Clinton: Will She Change Your Life?" In the article inside, the answer was "perhaps." According to the writer, journalist Gail Collins, "men are beginning to admit that we just might be as intelligent as they are"—a message congenial to the magazine's target readership of twenty-one- to forty-nine-year-old women. *Newsweek* offered Hillary Rodham Clinton, the lawyer/wife who reclaimed her maiden name and became Superwoman. "She's the working mother, trying to juggle a career, a child, a husband, a role, all at the same time, 24 hours a day," reported the writer, Sally Quinn.

Every political campaign tries to control the coverage it receives and force the press to carry its single chosen theme of the day. Because the modern presidency has become a continuation of electoral politics, the White House uses the tools of access available to it to control this message between elections. Its aim is to win over voters and get reelected; but the media also seek reelection by their "voters"—every day for a talk show or newspaper, weekly for magazines or television. From the managers' point of view, the Hillary Rodham Clinton story had a happy ending on election day: plucky presidential spouse wrests daily message from press and again gains control of image. "During the campaign she was defined by others: the press or the Republicans," remembered Margaret Carlson, who covered the Clintons for *Time* magazine. "Now she is defining herself."

This was true only up to a point. While the White House routinely used photo ops, made-for-television town meetings, and other staged events to assert control over the Clinton image, the press never stopped attempting to define Hillary Clinton for its own purposes. The myth of the master who tries to remake his subject in his own image, for self-centered reasons, is a familiar one. George Bernard Shaw slyly borrowed the Greek legend of Galetea and Pygmalion for his popular 1913 play about Professor Higgins ("the sculptor") and Eliza Doolittle ("the material"). In 1957, the composers Lerner and Lowe borrowed from the myth and created the musical, "My Fair Lady." On Broadway, Eliza, the Cockney flower girl, was transformed into a well-bred Englishwoman, and the manipulative Higgins into a warm, cuddly fellow. In the Washington real-life version of "My Fair Lady," there were no mutual makeovers and no happy ending.

The earliest Hillary Clinton coverage was likely to be conventional. Syndicated columnist and TV commentator Clarence Page set down the long-standing unwritten rules for spouses of political candidates.[6] The first sign that the "political wife" narrative was breaking out of its traditional form appeared when the press' treatment of Hillary Clinton itself became a story. The *Washington Post* reported that the Clinton campaign was engaged in an "internal tug-of-war over how to divide Mrs. Clinton's policymaking and cookie-baking roles." Elizabeth Neuffer in the *Boston Globe* referred to the "retooled" Hillary Clinton, while the *New York Times'* Alessandra Stanley talked of Mrs. Clinton's "fine-tuned" public persona. Joan Beck of the *Chicago Tribune,* among others, was reminded of the "Stepford Wives."

If the Supreme Court is said to follow the election returns, so too, does the Washington press corps. After the election, the coverage of Hillary Clinton took a friendly turn. *Time* magazine presented a sympathetic portrait of a "different kind of First Lady," while *Newsweek* wrote of the "team presidency" and called Mrs. Clinton the "First Lady plus." Also in *Time,* Margaret Carlson's "Hillary Clinton: Partner as Much as Wife," referred to its subject as an "amalgam of Betty Crocker, Mother Teresa and Oliver Wendall Holmes." The *New York Times* picked up on the Betty Crocker theme, assigning one of its food writers, Marian Burros, to produce "Hillary Clinton's New Home: Broccoli's In, Smoking's Out." The Burros article appeared on the front page of the *Times* with an eye-catching photograph showing Hillary Clinton in a Donna Karan gown, pretending to set the table before the Clintons' first official dinner. In the *Washington Post* "Style" section, Martha Sherrill offered a three-part series called "The Education of Hillary Clinton." The series detailed her journey from middle-class Republican suburbia to the White House, or as the *Post* sub-headline put it, "Goldwater Girl to First Lady." The series devoted one paragraph to Hillary Clinton's work with the Rose law firm in Little Rock and two paragraphs to her legal writings, while changes in her hairstyle and clothes garnered twelve paragraphs. Nothing was said of Hillary Clinton's work as chair of the Federal Legal Services Corporation from the late 1970s to the early 1980s. By way of defense, Sherrill said that she was reacting to the media—to the coverage of Hillary Clinton's hair and makeup. "What I tried to say was that people were critical of her appearance but really wanted to criticize something else." That "something else," Sherrill suggested, had to do with the electorate's inchoate feelings about women who looked "too strong" or "too intelligent."

Since then, Hillary Clinton has become a main news-section story, as likely to be covered by beat reporters as by style writers. Before the election, a typical article on Hillary Clinton would follow the model of *Newsweek*'s "First Lady Culture Clash." Eleanor Clift contrasted Barbara Bush, with her "homey figure and trademark white hair," and Hillary Clinton, the "hard-charging professional who doesn't usually settle for a supporting role." After the election, the contrasts were drawn between Hillary Clinton and elected political powers. On ABC's *Nightline,* correspondent Chris Bury reported that in one three-month period Hillary Clinton "outscored" Vice President Al Gore on the three networks' nightly newscasts. She appeared in a total of fifty-two minutes; he just four. In *USA Today,* columnist Joe Urschel updated "the Al-Hillary scoreboard," reporting that Hillary Clinton received 197 mentions in *USA Today* to 70 for Gore. For the *Washington Post,* the figures were Clinton: 282, Gore: 111. The male audience of right-wing talk and the women readers of the *Ladies Home Journal* were both likely to follow the score to see who was winning in the battle of the sexes.

Writers assigned to the Clintons acknowledged the new attention to such scorekeeping. There was a time, Maureen Dowd of the *New York Times* remembered, "when I used to follow Nancy Reagan around Kuala Lampur and report that she said, 'Isn't this lovely . . .' Certainly there's been a shift from that." While other presidents' wives—Nancy Reagan most recently—exerted great influence inside the White House, Dowd added, "Hillary Rodham Clinton is the first to be forthright about it."

Hillary Rodham Clinton's spousal role in such matters as domestic policy and health-care reform also carried demographic weight. The target audiences were ready to move on from, respectively, the femi-nazi and the Superwoman images: caricatures soon lose their power to provoke reactions. Galetea was resculpted again by her various Pygmalions. She was reduced to just one more familiar political figure on the conservative talk-radio circuit, a tired liberal. In the mainstream style sections, she became just one more successful professional woman. According to Margaret Carlson, "we got Hillary Clinton, but we could have gotten ten others like her. It's a generational shift." The full-time "helpmate wife" is political history—"there will be no more Barbara Bushes, that's over," says Carlson. Other potential candidates' wives, such as Elizabeth Dole and Marilyn Quayle, also are intelligent, high-achieving women and lawyers. On the left and right, Hillary Clinton has been relocated to familiar demographic ground. "Compared to some accomplished, professional friends of mine," said Martha Sherrill, thirty-four, "Hillary Clinton is quite conventional." In the Shaw play and Lerner-Lowe musical, that was how the free-spirited Eliza Doolittle turned out.

"Crazy . . . Just Crazy for You": Perot, Gingrich, and the New Suburban Majority

H. Ross Perot lost every campaign battle he has been in, yet somehow managed to win the wider political wars of the 1990s. As we noted, he ran his 1992 race for president "in the air," with appearances on *Larry King Live* and other talk shows and with thirty-minute infomercials, complete with visual aids to push home his bromidic message. He became the first man to enter campaign cyberspace, a candidate resolutely antiprint and, intellectually, antilinear.[1] As the historian Garry Wills pointed out, Perot avoids the press until something bad is about to be written about him; then, in defiance of logic, "he mounts a blitz, showing up on every talk show to distract people with charges against someone else."[2] First, he drawled on about George Bush; next, Bill Clinton; then the deficit, then the budget, then NAFTA. His campaign group, United We Stand America, claimed to reflect the feelings of grassroots Americans, with decentralized structure and bottom-up leadership: an anti-organization organization. A better name for it, one that reflected its top-down authority, would have been United We Stand Perot. One of Perot's closest aides, Orson Swindle, resigned from the group in disgust, telling a reporter that Perot "encouraged everybody to be heard, and then didn't have the capacity to listen."

Perot's organization fielded very few candidates, either in 1992 or, later, in the off-year races of 1994. This was because it was Perot himself who was the show. In 1992, he garnered 19 million votes in the process of running third behind Bush and Clinton. Two years later, the Republican House leadership, borrowing key tenets of its "Contract with America" from the Perot canon, swept into power. President Clinton, meanwhile, was doing a very good Perot imitation, holding Perot-style town meetings, complete with citizen questioners and statewide television hookups. Clinton also borrowed generously from the Perot song book, complaining about the unnamed "powerful forces" that make it hard for him to do the job the American public had elected him to do. What is more, the Clinton of 1994 displayed some of the same personal, persecution-complex mannerisms of the 1992-model Perot. Listening to Clinton at a Cranston, Rhode Island town meeting in the spring of 1994, *Time* magazine columnist Hugh Sidey found echoes of Perotista whining in the presidential dialogue. Sidey's commentary carried the headline "H. Ross Clinton?"

Both men, Perot and the faux-Perot, Clinton, were too intelligent not to be aware of what was going on. Responding to the various stories about his oversized ego and unstable behavior, Perot adopted the Patsy Cline country anthem "Crazy" at his rallies. On television, he danced with one of his daughters to the music. Clinton himself slyly sent up his carefully cultivated reputation as "one of us," a good ole boy, with a leering story about the astroturf carpeting he had installed in the back of his pickup truck (before he was married to Hillary Rodham, he added).

Even the tone-deaf could pick up populist Perotista themes throughout Clinton's and Gingrich's Washington. In the winter of 1994–95, the National Endowment for the Humanities (NEH) sponsored a series of televised town meetings across the country to create "a national conversation" aimed at countering ethnic, racial, and class divisions in America. These meetings were preceded by a series of nontelevised conferences involving foundations and academics called together to work up to the TV stage—essentially, conversations about The Conversation. The federal agency share of the cost was $1 million. The plan was easy to deride; one critic argued that the idea of "national conversation" itself was a contradiction in terms. But the NEH chairman, Dr. Sheldon Hackney, was firmly behind the town meetings, which came with the blessing of President Clinton.[3] Perot, of course, had been the leading proponent of electronic democracy to restore the American dream. "If we ever put the people back in charge of this country and make sure they understand the issues," he said, "you'll see the White House and Congress, like a ballet, pirouetting around the stage and getting things done in unison."[4]

At the other end of the social spectrum, generationally distinct from Perot and Hackney, was *Wired,* the magazine of the new multimedia culture. *Wired* wrote approvingly of electronic town meetings (ETMs). It reported on a health-care ETM held in mid-1993 via the interactive cable system of San Antonio, Texas. Subscribers used special software and set-top boxes "to send signals upstream," for example, by using their keypad to signify, "I disagree with that." Soon, around Washington, *Wired* became the hip, new read, approvingly quoted in the *Washington Post;* at least a half dozen White House staff members were listed as subscribers.

The imitation of faux populism by the Clinton administration was the least of it. The White House also participated in the anointment of outsider Perot as its opposition, a far bigger favor. Typically, the elevation of the pop entertainer Perot, occurred in the soft-media formats. Typically, too, the defining episode in this process was misread as a defeat for Perot, when it actually advanced his abiding cause.

The lost-battle/won-war moment came when Perot appeared with Vice President Al Gore on *Larry King Live* in November 1993. The occasion of their joint performance was a televised debate on the merits of legislation in support of the North American Free Trade

Agreement, then pending in Congress. The press's metaphor machinery went into overdrive at the prospect of the Gore-Perot meeting. Among the most frequently used pop-cult images were: the boxing-ring cliché ("Big Brawl," according to *Newsweek*); the military/western cliché (*Newsday*'s "Border War" and "High Noon at the Larry King Corral"); and the gambling cliché ("Clinton Betting that Public Has Tired of Texan", the *New York Times*). In the end, the prize-fight image won. "NAFTA Goes a Full 15 Rounds," the *Los Angeles Times* editorial page decided, while David Broder in the *Washington Post* concluded that "Gore had the better of the brawl." Syndicated columnist William Safire agreed: "Gore Flattens Perot." Less than thirty-six hours after Larry King bid his CNN audience goodnight, Herblock in the *Washington Post* sketched Perot prone on a boxing-ring apron; the *New York Times*' Anna Quindlen wrote about Perot in the past tense ("Mr. Perot had a purpose in American politics for a fleeting moment during the last presidential election").

Perot had been pronounced finished in print before, only to bounce up again, a populist Punchinello. As such, he was part of the long comeback tradition in American public life; recent examples include Richard Nixon, defeated by John Kennedy in 1960, only to win election and reelection in 1968 and 1972, and Ronald Reagan, rejected as a candidate by his party in 1976, and then its nominee and winner in 1980 and 1984. In the 1990s, comebacks were made easier as a result of the new media environment. In the wired nation, Perot did not need a history, a party, a platform, or even a record of consistency. Instead, he could tap into the vague discontent and free-floating anger of some subset of the population, whose voice could be amplified by the talk shows and pressure-group campaigns. The National Rifle Association, for example, has become expert at generating faxes and phone calls from its members to "targeted" senators and representatives.

Perot's continued political leverage was guaranteed by the same Washington system he regularly derided. He nominated himself to play a spoiler role in the races of 1994 and 1996 on the basis of the fact that in 1992 he received more than 20 percent of the vote in no fewer than 221 congressional districts; in 76 of those districts, mainly in the small towns and suburbs of the South and West, his vote share rose to over 25 percent. The figures did not give him a single seat in the House or Senate. But they strikingly demonstrated the power of the Perot "swing vote." These numbers were read intently by Newt Gingrich, who fashioned his "Contract with America" accordingly. Gingrich understood that Republican candidates in the November 1994, elections would need Perot voters to oust the Democratic incumbents. The Perot numbers also impressed the political journalists. According to Hal Bruno, political director at ABC News, "Perot empowered Perot. He has become a serious force in American politics." Actually, Perot became a national political factor because the media system had empowered him as well. He figured out the media's needs and offered them his countryisms and his good visuals. In the Gore-Perot debate, Perot's deployment of photographs showing Mexican workers' shanties—see the poverty of the people we are linking our economy to—made for better television than Gore's mug shots of Smoot and Hawley, the 1920s trade protectionists. No matter that Perot cavalierly slandered a neighboring nation. In addition, Perot and his staff consciously improved their media relations. The unreliable, unresponsive, who-needs-the-press attitude of his campaign in 1992 was replaced by a professional operation that ran on time and was less confrontational. On camera, Perot remained resolutely hostile, playing to his constituency's prejudices about Big Media. "They used to give you very little information," Hal Bruno remembered. "Now, your fax machine is flooded with Perot's schedule." More than twangy sound bites and newly efficient news-management techniques aided Perot, however. When our News Study Group at NYU assembled and analyzed some 400 of Perot's newspaper and news magazine stories, as well as television clips since the beginning of the Clinton administration, we found ample evidence of how Perot came to be treated as the effective opposition to the administration rather than as an entertaining gadfly or failed third-party candidate.[5]

Perot benefited from the reflexive practices of the permanent campaign. Both traditional political journalism and the newer formats of the soft media are committed to "campaign news" after the campaign is over. At the core of this coverage is the binary model of the election-year horse race: two contestants, two positions, charge-countercharge, rebuttal-*re*-rebuttal. But in the case of several administration policy initiatives, such as health care and NAFTA, the two-sided model did not apply. The argument was much more fluid; Democrats and Republicans, conservatives and liberals, neos and paleos, found themselves taking one of several sides in the debate. Such issues confounded the press's model of political coverage. Neither Bob Dole nor Newt Gingrich had yet emerged as majority leaders, and so someone else had to fill the "other side" role in an election-style contest. Old and new media alike elected Perot the all-purpose opposition spokesman. Inevitably, then, Larry King presented "Gore vs. Perot: The Debate." The Clintonites described their decision to send Gore up against Perot as a gamble. More accurately, it was an implicit acknowledgment of the role that the entertainment formats had already helped create for Perot. Perot was not the chief presidential contender during the Clinton administration; but he *acted* like a candidate. The call-in formats and mainstream press both accepted the fiction, for example, treating his half-truths and crackpot assertions about "giant sucking sounds" as if they constituted a serious analysis of trade policy.[6]

The White House decided to go along with the election-year model, judging it needed all the help it could get for NAFTA: an erratic opponent with loopy arguments certainly made the selling job easier. The tactic paid off; NAFTA was passed. Perot lost the battle. In the long run, however, Perot's permanent campaign was legitimized. The newspaper clips and television coverage show that

Perot's endless campaign resumed the day Clinton's inaugural bunting was taken down from Washington's street lights. Naturally, it is an ETM candidacy: carefully staged rallies for the faithful, combined with frequent appearances on the nightly cable talk shows and the morning network news programs. Television producers justified Perot's semipermanent guest status with circular reasoning. He has "a willingness to say something . . . [to stand] in the middle of the ring," explained Tamara Haddad, producer of *Larry King Live* until she left to go to ABC. According to Lane Vernados, a vice president at CBS News in New York, it was simple: "Perot is an available son of a gun." In fact, Perot's availability was largely confined to television, where he was cast, election-style, as the voice of the Clinton opposition—TV has little patience and almost no time for a many-sided presentation. Whenever the Clintonites stumbled, Perot showed up to hitch a free ride on television. After Clinton's infamous $200 haircut troubles, for example, Perot called a news conference, supposedly to criticize the coverage. But while Perot was chiding reporters for diverting public attention from substance, he was simultaneously channeling media attention to himself. Print reporters were confined to writing about what Perot did on television.

In permanent-campaign mode, Perot's twenty-four-hour "Media Update Line" provided a daily telephone account of his scheduled appearances, the majority of them nontraditional ETM dates on television and radio. The same week he appeared with Gore on *Larry King Live,* Perot did a Tampa rally carried by C-SPAN and a radio call-in broadcast on talk host Chuck Harder's *For the People.* Print reporters were invited to listen. "You can't interview him, there's no access," complained Debbie Howlett, who covered Perot for *USA Today.* If the 1992 Perot campaign did not exist in a physical sense, the ETM mode remains the vehicle for Perot's ambitions. His Dallas headquarters published a checklist for supporters planning a local Perot rally. The instructions were designed to produce a camera-ready ETM event, as scripted as any

TV movie-of-the-week. The site should be "in a safe part of town located as near as possible to our supporters." Auditoriums should be of modest size (to appear full for the camera); the security should not be on stage, storm trooper fashion, but rather scattered inconspicuously behind the crowd. The band should know how to play "Crazy" and "The Star Spangled Banner." Perot wanted his suburban audience to be comfortable: they were part of the show *as seen on TV*. Not so crazy after all.[7]

On those occasions when Perot granted a newspaper interview, it was usually in the form of a teleconference call; reporters were permitted to ask one question each, with no opportunity for a follow-up. This strategy allowed Perot to broadcast his message without losing control. It was also more cost effective from the Texas tycoon's business point of view; in the standard interview, Perot fretted, you might spend a lot of time with a reporter or columnist and "have no idea how it will play in the paper." Virtual conferencing also kept press undesirables locked out. When the *Dallas Morning News* criticized his opposition to NAFTA in an editorial, Perot took the position that he had no time to "debate little groups like the *News*." Perhaps in retaliation, the print commentaries tended to be negative after Perot's television performances. Such criticism was not likely to change the frequency of Perot's appearances. The ratings for *Larry King Live* the night of the NAFTA debate increased tenfold. CNN had not had an audience that size since the Gulf War.

A year later, Newt Gingrich became a new Perot, or rather a *real* Perot, rounding up suburban voters in the congressional elections to craft a Republican majority. Gingrich arrived just in time, mediawise. The Perot Show was repetitious, a TV rerun: journalism's fight model needed freshening. Gingrich, learned child of the publicity age, played new, old, and hyper media skillfully; he went online and on MTV ("Newt: Raw," the music channel called the Speaker's shrewdly promoted interview with twentysomethings). In New Hampshire, he and Bill Clinton answered questions at a seniors' picnic: two chubby white men jockeying for the populist center, while C-SPAN carried the event live.

The phoniness of such populism is apparent when contrasted with the real thing. Harry S Truman came out of the American heartland, plain speaking and committed to upholding "traditional values." He scoffed at high-hats as much as the next little guy. Truman's biographers, from Merle Miller to David McCulloch, were unanimous: what you saw was what you got. The late mayor Richard J. Daley of Chicago once described his career as he wanted to be remembered: one wife, one life. That applied equally to Truman. Although Truman often evoked the name of "the people" during his presidency, he did not presume that he alone could interpret its will. He never relied on public opinion sampling or lost any sleep over his standing in the polls. On April 11, 1951, in the middle of the unpopular Korean War, Commander in Chief Truman decided he had to remove the insubordinate General Douglas MacArthur, a godlike figure as popular in the polls as Truman was unpopular. In the White House meetings leading up to Truman's decision, not a word was said about polls, public opinion, the press, or the pundits.[8]

Loyalty to party and faith in government animated Truman's politics. When party affiliation and shared history have little to do with politics, however, something else has to take their place. As was the case with the Perot virtual candidacy, individual personality more and more occupies the center stage. With the emphasis on the personal, the balance between the private sphere and public life has shifted, and what was once considered personal has become public. Approving critics now argue that radio and TV talk shows, along with their upscale interactive versions, E-mail and computer bulletin boards, have taken the place of the backyard-fence chatter of an earlier era. Whether this restores a shared sense of community, as these same boosters claim, is not clear. The new American chatter has given wider public circulation to many of the same topics that neighbors usually share, such as innuendoes about sex, money, and antic behavior ("maybe that guy really is crazy?"). The public airing of what were once private matters, not so incidentally, crowds the stage of politics with players who in the past were in the background.

Once again, Larry King's show provided a stage for the new personality politics. Early in the 1992 presidential campaign, Judith Campbell Exner, a ghostly image of the 1960s, appeared on TV sets tuned to CNN. She was fifty-eight at the time of her appearance, dressed in slacks, a blue blazer, and a white blouse. Her spinal cancer had progressed, she told King, and so she was on borrowed time—as well as from another time. Beneath the grandmotherly resigned demeanor, however, a viewer could still imagine the knowing eyes and pouty good looks: the face and figure that had attracted the equally cool glance of a youthful presidential candidate named John F. Kennedy one night in Las Vegas, thirty-two years before. Exner had told her pulp-novel story before: mafia moll and mistress of the president of the United States; courier of cash payments intended to buy the 1960 West Virginia Democratic primary; go-between for a White House plan to use the Chicago mob to eliminate Fidel Castro. It had all come out in 1975. Yet her appearance on CNN in 1992 could not have been more timely. She offered a case study in the argument about the press's role in covering the private lives of public officials. Gennifer Flowers was no Judith Campbell, and Bill Clinton may not be a Jack Kennedy. But the Washington press dozed through Judy and Jack, missing two years of phone calls, around-the-clock FBI stakeouts, and coast-to-coast liaisons.

Eight presidential terms later, the public and the press were wracked by doubts about that graduate-seminar standby, "the press's role in covering the private lives of public people." A strain of hypocrisy ran through the discussion, as obvious as the roots of Flowers's hair. Flowers and, later, Paula Jones, were both burdened by their downmarket image; in the eyes of the Big Media elite, one was a failed lounge singer, the other a $10,500-a-year clerk. Worse, they each had a momentary stake in promoting their stories. Flowers had accepted $100,000 from the supermarket tabloid *Star* for her tale: Cash for trash. Pornographers are trying to "hijack democracy . . . the media . . . have now taken up residence in the gutter," *Boston Globe* columnist Thomas Oliphant complained. The same day, a *Globe* editorial offered a more sensible position. "If Flowers had been paid $100,000 to write her memoirs for Simon & Schuster" the editorial noted, "and if those memoirs included an assertion that she had an affair with Clinton, no newspaper would have worried that money was involved with deciding whether to report her story."

These struggles between the candidate and the press, and among the contending elite media and trash media, were about the forms that contemporary political coverage can take. Every four years, the journalists arrive prepared to fight the previous presidential campaign and to box with shadows that go back to the 1960s, and shades of Judith Exner and John Kennedy.

For decades, a clubby, relatively small group of reporters *was* the political press. The boys on Tim Crouse's bus, as we have seen, wore proper suits and ties, shared confidences, and mingled more or less fraternally with the candidates. The beau ideal of the political journalist was Theodore H. White, lover of "the process" and a friend of the men he covered. In the enduring image of White, he is seated in a sedan with Jack Kennedy, an advance man, and a driver, rolling over the black-tops of West Virginia. No single reporter since has had that kind of access: too many important egos would be offended if excluded. Further, the size of the campaign press has increased a hundredfold. Today, anyone with camera equipment or a plausible story can show up at any political event, claiming to be "press, on assignment." In May 1994, Gennifer Flowers held a news conference in New York to promote the two-cassette set of her Clinton conversations, available to the public by calling a 1-800 number and placing an order. A newshound "representing" the radio shock-jock Howard Stern appeared, along with 200 other self-described journalists, as well as representatives from Italian, Japanese, and Spanish television. At an earlier news conference, Stern's man had asked Flowers, on behalf of the morning drive-time audience, "Did Governor Clinton wear a condom?"—a line that was quickly picked up and replayed around the country, even by other news organizations with their own correspondents at the Flowers conference.

The old Club could do nothing about the Stern gang. But changed as it is, the Club enforced certain standards of deportment for members using the library or dining rooms. Several major news organizations, including the *Washington Post,* the *Los Angeles Times,* and the *Boston Globe,* dispatched reporters to Little Rock to check out the recurring rumors of Clinton's infidelities, as well as other details of his biography. Eventually, the *Times* found evidence deemed firm enough for publication; much of this material was gleaned from a lawsuit brought by an ex-Arkansas official who had feuded with then-Governor Clinton. The suit had been on file in the U.S. District Court in Little Rock since October 25, 1990. Typically, the Club members shared these frissions first with each other, and only later with their readers or viewers. The audience could only guess at the games being played when Washington reporter Cokie Roberts, the moderator of a Democratic candidates' debate in January 1992, asked Clinton to comment on "stories about your private life."

Star—the trash tabloid—sent its own snoopers to Little Rock. They rang doorbells, heard tales of denial from several of the women named in the suit (or from the women's lawyers), and kept leaning on the bell, just like real, mainstream reporters—if not quite in the tradition of Woodward and Bernstein. Persistence and $100,000 paid off; *Star* produced Flowers, one of the women named in the suit, plus her tapes of phone conversations with Clinton. "Was it news? Hell, yes," said Jerry Nachman, then-editor of the *New York Post*. He could not afford to send his own reporter to Arkansas but played the *Star's* materials on the *Post's* front page. "Journalism normally reports on the contents of law suits," Nachman explained, and added: "You're changing the rules if you say that, before we report a law suit, we have to verify its allegations." The other New York City tabloids, *Newsday* and the *News*, put the story of Flowers and her tapes on their front pages, too. When Clinton denied that he had had an affair with Flowers, although acknowledging that he had talked to her, the tabloids' narrative wrote itself. *Newsday* and the *News* produced identical headlines: "Sex, Lies and Audiotape." The elite press, including the *New York Times*, the *Los Angeles Times*, and the *Washington Post*, placed the first stories well inside their papers.

Conservative columnist Charles Krauthammer took this as a welcome sign of newfound press responsibility. The front pages of the *New York Times* and the *Washington Post*, Krauthammer argued (echoing what Jack Nelson had told us; see chapter 4), set the national news agenda; they tell other journalists "what's important" as well as "what's respectable." Four years earlier, candidate Gary Hart shot himself in the foot—and higher—when he challenged reporters suspicious of his infidelities to follow him. Almost too easily, the *Miami Herald's* snoopers uncovered the story of Hart and Donna Rice and their adventures aboard a yacht with the tabloid-perfect name, *Monkey Business*. Although Krauthammer conceded that the Rice story may have belonged on the elites' front pages in 1988 because Hart's behavior was "compulsive and/or current," since then "a consensus appears to be developing: if it happened a long time ago in a galaxy far, far away, then it's a minor trespass."

That was one way to look down on Flowers, Jones, et al. It implied that the Club knew best, and that the new members should take their cues from their elders. An elite "consensus" would decide what the voting public should be told, when it should be told, and how. Stories of sex and lies were suitable only for the dim, unwashed audience of *Star*. Consensus, however, has given way to the demands of competition, and different news organizations respond differently. On its January 24, 1992, campaign-coverage page, the *New York Times* ran a stealth story about Clinton and Flowers—eight inches in length, unsigned, and tucked in the bottom right-hand corner of an inside page ("Clinton Denounces New Report of Affair"). By contrast, the *Washington Post,* on the same day, carried a thorough, well-balanced forty-three-inch story, with a two-column photograph and a double byline on page A8 ("Clinton Calls Tabloid Report of 12 Year Affair 'Not True'"). The old order passes, slowly. A. M. Rosenthal in his *Times* op-ed column a few days later praised the news editors at the *Times,* as it happens, his successors, "for playing the [Clinton] story exactly right." That is, "they reported the episode, because to ignore it entirely would have been journalistically pretentious. But they kept the reports conspicuously brief. Disdain for the poison-pen press and its emulators leapt deliciously from the page."

Some part of the elites' discomfort with the poison-pen journalists was due to a reversal of roles. The Club was accustomed to having the political story for itself; the small fish swam in its wake. In the 1990s, the Club faced the prospect of picking from among the leftovers. With allowances for some details, Hart-Rice was the checkout-counter magazine version of Clinton-Flowers. In 1988, the unfortunate couple was part of a morality play known in that mainstream media as "the character issue." As it was explained at the time: "If (name of candidate) cannot handle (nature of transgression), then how can voters trust him in the White House when he's dealing with (category of serious problem: the economy, Japan, whatever)." In 1988, too, the best case for the mainstream press's pursuit of character was made by Max Frankel, then the executive editor of the *Times* (and the man Rosenthal praised for restraint). In a memo to his staff on the eve of the campaign, Frankel defended the *Times'* editors decision to explore the private conduct of candidates, who "have paraded their wives and families and fidelity to family values before the public, by way of claiming certain character and personality traits." Frankel added: "When these claims turn fraudulent, they are as noteworthy as any other serious misrepresentation to the electorate." The case for disclosure could rest with that summary. But the 1990s' Clintons, speedier by half than the 1980s' Hart model, took the offensive and evoked a "zone of privacy." It worked for a time. The *New York Times* quoted Clinton's jab at the "intrusive press." *U.S. News & World Report* credited the candidate with "defusing the bombshell." The syndicated columnist Ellen Goodman suggested there were "two different sets of moral attitudes" in America: An older religious right worried about sin, and younger moderns concerned about "relationships" and the "wife's pain." The Clintons emerged in Goodman's column with the secularists' vote.

Some of the elites appeared to be most pained by the thought that they were losing "their" candidate, the leader committed to needed change, the New Democrat, the man who, above all else, seemed electable. Jimmy Breslin, tabloid writer and urban populist, was among the first to poke a big hole in the Clinton myth. Listening to the Clinton-Flowers tapes, Breslin picked up on a key exchange, the moment when Flowers said to Clinton, "Do you remember what I said to you?" Breslin, thanks to the time he spent around the criminal courts in Brooklyn and Queens, recognized the cue, as any eighteen-year-old thief would. It was the "lead sentence of the rodent. Always, the 'do you remember' is said in the presence of recording equipment or a stool pigeon." But Bill Clinton, Yale lawyer, Rhodes scholar, presumptive leader of the free world, answered: "No, what'd you say?" (Then followed some dirty talk by Flowers.) No one in the Club bothered to pass on Breslin's insight: Clinton did not have the street sense to beat a stolen-auto charge.

Efforts to frame Clinton-Flowers or Clinton-Jones in terms of class standing, good taste, or a prurience quotient produced mixed results. University of Virginia government professor Larry Sabato worried about the attention the stories were getting. The news media were "pandering to the lowest common denominator of the American public," Sabato declared. The public "lacks civic education"—large numbers of Americans know little of the "important issues of the day" and have no real desire to learn more. Perhaps, but one shortcircuiting of civic education begins when editors decide at their page-one meetings that inquiries into the candidate's finances, for example, are important while those about the candidate's sex life are not. Moreover, if party and ideology are now regarded as less important than character, all aspects of the candidate's personality become relevant to the presidency, from the amount of charitable deductions taken to bedroom behavior.

In the early days of the modern television presidency, John F. Kennedy projected an image of grace and intellect. Reporters and editors who knew of, or suspected, Kennedy's olympiad of sexual athleticism kept the information from their audiences. In the spirit of the old Fleet Street expression, journalists saved their best stories for after-hours, to tell each other. Some of the younger journalists who were around in the 1960s occupied positions of authority in the 1990s. Belatedly, some have recognized their own complaisant roles. The Kennedy stories continued to trickle out, completing a section of the historical record. The public managed to absorb the information and move forward. In any case, new rules governed the press-candidate relationship. While no one ever accused Dan Quayle of an excess of wisdom, the then-vice president, or his advisers, had the right sound bite prepared for reporters who asked him about the Clinton sex stories. "When you run for president or vice president," Quayle said, "you just got to expect everything's going to be discussed, whether it's fair or unfair." Neither Quayle nor anyone else, however, was prepared for the Niagara-like level of noise that regularly thundered over America in the mid-1990s.

Virtual America

During the 1993–94 television season, a group of Republican operatives, led by the long-time Washington activist Paul Weyrich, started the National Empowerment Television (NET), a broadcast service dedicated to promoting a Reaganesque view of the world. While its message is conservative, NET should not be confused with another right-thinking channel, the Christian Broadcasting Network (CBN). The Christian Broadcasting Network is led by the Reverend Pat Robertson, the noted religious broadcaster—a description he preferred to the more pejorative term, televangelist—and once and future Republican candidate for president. Robertson's CBN features his *700 Club* with its mix of news, commentary, and inspirational talk from a studio: unfashionably retro, the *700 Club* uplinked only. NET, however, promised interactive call-in segments and ample on-air access for conservative affinity groups; the National Rifle Association, for example, supplied regular programming.

Not long after NET began broadcasting, another veteran Republican operator, the political consultant Douglas Bailey, announced plans for the American Political Channel (APC), a cable-TV service devoted to political news shows, town meetings with elected officials, viewers' call-ins and other interactive programming. The stated aim of APC, Bailey explained, was "to give access to people who've never had access before"—left or right, Christian or heathen, empowered or frustrated. In addition to *Town Meeting America*—the title explains the program——the APC schedule called for *Feet to the Fire* (the opportunity for home viewers to phone in their questions to cabinet members and other Washington officials); *Playing in Peoria* (how governmental policy matters were being received in the American heartland, beyond insular Washington); and *Video Soapbox* (videotaped contributions from viewers, responding to the invitation to make their own, short political speeches, using home camcorders). The channel was determined to be resolutely tri-partisan, with an advisory panel that included David Wilhelm, then the Democratic National Committee chair; Haley Barbour, his Republican counterpart, and a representative to be named by Ross Perot.

The American Political Channel was conceived as a for-profit enterprise, with air time sold to political parties and lobbying groups. As usual in these image-conscious days, it came wrapped in the bright packaging of "electronic democracy." With the new channel, according to Bailey, "there will be no excuse for a member of Congress not to hold long-distance [televised] town meetings." But members of Congress already had access to the voters, and the voters to their representatives and senators. C-SPAN 1 and 2, the no-frills, no-commercials cable networks, were supported by cable-system operators throughout the country; they transmitted all the floor business of the U.S. House of Representatives and the Senate. When the House and Senate were not in session, C-SPAN regularly broadcast congressional hearings, Washington news conferences, a daily viewer call-in show, town meetings, speeches, conventions, academic symposia and seminars, and special series (for example, the quadrennial *Road to the White House,* and *Book Notes* on Sunday evenings). Brian Lamb, C-SPAN's founder and impassive host on its call-in shows, hoped by the late 1990s to introduce C-SPAN 3, 4, and 5, devoted to domestic politics, business and economic topics, and international affairs.

Initially, technology drove these developments. New channel space became available with each physical expansion of the cable universe; by industry estimates, there were forty-one national channels in 1983 and more than double that number ten years later. The new digital-compression technology theoretically makes possible 100-plus channel systems by the time of 1996 presidential campaign. The economics of broadcasting is another matter. In early 1994, the Federal Communications Commission (FCC) ordered cuts in the rates that cable-system operators can charge their customers. Arguing that they no longer have any financial incentive to add new channels, the operators began lobbying to get the FCC regulations overturned. Their tactics were time-tested: unless the government relented, the operators argued, the consumers would suffer, deprived of their cable cornucopia. No one doubted that this kind of threat would be effective; "relief" will be granted, sooner rather than later, and the crybaby lords of cable will find the needed pennies for new programming in a cookie jar they had previously overlooked.

Political exchanges between the governors and the governed and ideology-based "empowerment" programs will be only a small part of the expected proliferation of cable programming. The same 1993–94 season that brought the start of the NET and the announcement of APC also saw the birth of the ESPN-2 channel, designed to carry those third-ranked sports events that were not quite up to the appeal of the games on the parent networks, ABC or ESPN-1. In the spring of 1994, the Television Food Network (TVFN) began cablecasting, featuring news, information, and interactive talk about eating. Donna Hanover Guiliani, the wife of the mayor of New York City, was one of the on-camera hosts. Some of the spirit of TVFN was captured by its founding executive, Reese Schoenfeld, when he called it "Larry King with a kitchen." In fact, TVFN made do without a King but with a Robin—Robin Leach, the oleaginous host of the 1980s' television series *Lifestyles of the Rich and Famous*. Leach's TVFN show, *Robin Leach Talking Food*, combined celebrity chatter with cooking.

Other announced additions, coming too late to be counted in the 1993–94 season, included the Health channel, the Sci-Fi channel, the Military channel, Turner Classic Movies, and the fX channel from Rupert Murdoch's Fox network. fX began in June 1994, with twenty-four hours of talk and entertainment programming, wearing its populist, interactive heart on its sleeve. The fX studio in New York City was designed to look like an expensive apartment. Viewers can "visit" its "rooms" by Internet, fax, or phone.

On July 4, 1994, NBC, operators of the cable network CNBC, introduced America's Talking, a channel devoted solely to talk and call-in shows. The patriotic launching was preceded by a shrewd publicity campaign based on another star-spangled ritual. A highly public search was conducted in each of the ten largest cities reached by the CNBC network for an ordinary citizen to be crowned host of his/her own CNBC talk show for one year—much like the reign of Miss America. The search garnered several days of publicity for CNBC for a modest investment; the new talk star was given a salary of $75,000 for a year's work. Like fX, America's Talking was quick to go interactive. In the summer of 1994, the cable network joined with Prodigy, one of the nation's largest online services, to allow viewers with computers to input questions and comments to program hosts. Computer monitors tuned to Prodigy were placed conspicuously on the sets of America's Talking.

No perceived taste has been left unsatisfied. At successive National Cable Television Association conventions in the summers of 1993 and 1994, industry members preparing for the world of 100-channel cable promoted two sound-alike networks, the Game Show channel from Sony, and the Game channel from International Family Entertainment. The Sony plan offered fresh made-for-cable game shows with human contestants. Its rival, after promising repeat broadcasts of network game shows, decided to focus instead on a Cable Health Club network. A third same-sounding venture, the Sega channel from the makers of Sega Genesis arcade games, featured video-game programming.[1] Weekend hackers have been promised the Arnold Palmer Golf channel (tournaments, tips, and talk); multimedia hackers already have the Computer network (more instructional chatter). Thoroughbred bettors can look forward to the Racing channel, the ultimate in interactivity: viewers call a 1-800 number, place their bets using credit cards, and then watch races simulcast from around the country. Among the new or planned ventures are the History channel and the Romance Classics network, featuring bodice-ripper movies. The Parents channel, the Pet Television network, the Classic Music channel, the World African network, the Independent Film channel, House and Garden Television, and the Outdoor Life channel—all are self-explanatory. Wait, there's more: a network offering classified ads exclusively, and the Booknet channel, which came with the imprimatur of E. L. Doctorow and promises of author interviews, publishing news and gossip, reviews, and readings. Perhaps the daftest idea of all involved the marriage of two proven cable systems, Generation X's MTV and QVC, their parents' home-shopping network. Viewers would be involved interactively, not once but twice on the channel: they could choose the music videos to be aired, watch and listen, and then phone in their record, video, or other music-related orders to a toll-free number.[2]

Behind the fantasists' high-minded talk about public service and the empowering qualities of interactive ventures is a familiar market-driven business plan. Cable has become a form of special-interest, or niche, broadcasting, much like radio before it. These niche appeals have earned recognition in the form of significant audiences and bottom-line profits for the so-called first-tier cable networks: the all-news CNN; ESPN with its big-ticket sports events; the premium HBO channel featuring upscale drama motion pictures; Arts & Entertainment's middlebrow series and documentaries; and, most spectacularly, MTV with its twenty-four hours of music and talk programming targeted to its eighteen to twenty-four year-old audience.

To the cable-system operators, profit-minded rather than empowerment fabulists, not all channels are equal. The system owners like programming that extracts extra payments from subscribers over and above the basic cable rates, for example, premium movies, pay-per-view entertainment events, and home-shopping services. But competition also complicates the business for the operators; as channels divided and multiplied like yeast cells, it became increasingly difficult to be seen or heard. As the new cable ventures struggled for viewers, the model of a new TV season each fall applied as well to the new multichannel universe. "Just as many new shows fail, so will many new channels fail," explains Larry Fraiberg, who ran independent television stations in New York on channels 5 and 9 for many years. Or more accurately, Fraiberg points out, the programming—the software—will fail. The hard-wired channel space will still be available.

Again, while technology made possible the 1990s' scramble for new programming, economic forces helped determine many of the outcomes. ABC, CBS, NBC, and Fox moved deeper into the development of new channels and new cable programming—and into direct competition with themselves—to protect their audience base from competitors. The broadcast networks spent most of the 1980s lobbying Congress to win backing in the regulatory fight with cable operators over retransmission rights. The broadcasters won the battle, but lost the war. Congress agreed to make cable systems compensate the broadcasters whose signals were being relayed; but the amount and form of compensation was left to marketplace negotiations. The cable-system operators faced down the networks, offering new channel space rather than cash or stock shares. One by one, the networks capitulated. Beginning in 1994, ABC, CBS, NBC, and Fox all began looking for twenty-four hours of software to fill their new cable channels, while still bearing the burden of finding programming for their original core franchises.[3]

ABC, with its ESPN connection, suffered the least. The 1980s demonstrated that young American males will watch anything involving a sphere. But the best strategy belonged to NBC; it recognized that product was essential. First, Robert Wright, the president of NBC, reached over to CBS to hire Andrew Lack as president of news. Lack was a producer of magazine shows—someone with day-to-day experience getting a product on the air. The NBC entertainment and sports divisions also were turned over to other software men, the producers Don Ohlmeyer and Dick Ebersol. Wright's boldest move came in early 1994, when he hired Roger Ailes to run the two NBC cable networks, the established CNBC and the new America's Talking network. The appointment caused some unease inside NBC because of Ailes's two decades of political work for conservative Republicans (Ailes made the television spots that helped three Republican presidents win their elections; at one time in the U.S. Senate, no fewer than fourteen incumbent Republican senators were the beneficiaries of Ailes's political consulting services). But the critics missed the real meaning of the Ailes appointment: he was a pure child of the media age, a professional producer who took up politics and not a political party operative who happens to know television. "My 20 year detour," he called his political work from the 1968 Nixon presidential campaign through the Reagan reelection campaign to George Bush's 1988 walkover. "It was great but it's over and I'm where I want to be, in the pit, producing."

Like Lack and the other NBC operating division presidents, Ailes knew the software. This experience dates back to the 1960s; he was the twenty-seven-year-old executive producer of the *Mike Douglas Show*—the equivalent in 1960s' popularity to *Oprah* today—when he met Richard Nixon. Ailes taught Nixon and, later, George Bush, almost all they needed to know about television (Ronald Reagan did not need any on-camera instruction, only the effective political spots Ailes made for him in 1984). Throughout these campaigns, Ailes kept producing theatrical shows on and off

Broadway, as well as television entertainment specials. He was also a consultant to Fortune 500 executives including NBC's Wright, while appearing regularly as a commentator on the *Today Show.* The network Ailes inherited was an awkward hybrid, the result of CNBC's merger with the old Financial News network. During the day, CNBC offered its money wheel—live financial news and interviews, with a continuous market ticker streaming across the bottom of the screen. At night, CNBC became a stream of words as constant as the ticker. The programming was a kind of archaeological excavation dig of talk: interview shows by 1970s-era figures Dick Cavett and Tom Snyder, a 1980s' cold war pairing of the all-American Phil Donahue and the ex-Soviet journalist Vladimir Pozner, and the very 1990s' *Equal Time,* a half hour of political talk and call-ins with women ideologues taking the part usually played by male host John McLaughlin of the *McLaughlin Group* (McLaughlin has his own interview show on the next half hour). At 11 P.M. sex talk took over, with Bob Berkowitz's popular interview show and call-in *Real Personal.*

Ailes believes in the expanding cable universe. Traditional broadcasters must adapt or perish. "This is the future," he says. "If you're just a milkman making home deliveries, one day a drive-through dairy appears and puts you out of business." He claims not to be worried about the prospect of viewers dispersed over 100 or more channels because niche programming will cater only to very narrow interests (according to Ailes, "400 channels will be offering Japanese brush-painting lessons"). Ailes himself is now one of the "narrowcasters," and some of the cable programming on America's Talking is almost as specialized as the brush-painting channel. NBC had the option of splitting the present CNBC schedule into one twenty-four-hour money wheel and moving the interview shows to the America's Talking channel. Instead, it opted for new programming. Some of the early shows crossed the line separating parody from "reality" so effortlessly that viewers had to keep reminding themselves they were *not* watching a skit on *Saturday Night*

Live. In the morning, *Am I Nuts?* offered two therapists who dispensed advice to callers while sitting in a studio set with padded walls. The prime of prime time was given over for a period to *Bugged,* featuring calls from viewers who were allowed to rant and rave from 8 to 9 P.M.

The unremitting drive for saleable program software to fill channel space inevitably affected the content of programming. Quality control was more difficult when so much product had to be processed. In fact, the idea of control itself seemed subversive to the spirit of the interactive age. The signature image of the call-in world was the sparkling on-air personality, not the dour, stickler editor or producer at an off-camera desk. The hosts, in any case, did not see themselves primarily as journalists; at most, they were curious questioners and sincere facilitators, and always entertaining. The callers, too, had to be entertaining. When flamers, blowhards who shoot out overheated rhetoric, become the norm for discourse, the minimal standards of fact-collecting, logical argument, and reasoned judgment are likely to suffer. Reality becomes "virtual reality," *a condition resembling truth but not truth itself.* Who has the time, or the inclination or intelligence, to dawdle over the old niceties like accuracy?

The spring of 1993 was a particularly receptive time for flaming. The talk shows and the mainstream news outlets alike transmitted several odd stories, including the virtual news that:

- Walt Disney was a special agent for the FBI who informed on his fellow Hollywood moviemakers.
- The Lindbergh baby kidnapping was a hoax, engineered by the Lone Eagle himself and his wife to cover up their complicity in the infant's accidental death.
- J. Edgar Hoover, the feared director of the Federal Bureau of Investigation, was a closet homosexual, who paraded around his

suite during parties at the Plaza Hotel in New York City wearing garter belts and dresses.

All of this hot stuff was contained in books from authentic publishers who printed on real paper, with actual fiberboard covers. These books and the news reports, tabloid TV segments, and radio talk inspired by them were protected by the First Amendment. The stories also enjoyed freedom from fact checkers, the pickers of nits who act to slow authors' overactive imaginations at many magazines and, to a lesser extent, at newspapers and in television news. Happily for the retellers of the Disney, Lindbergh, and Hoover stories, too, the principals were no longer around: dead men cannot sue. When such accounts appear, even when an announcement of their prospective appearance is made, this Mickey Mouse material immediately becomes "news." The way this happens helps explain why distrust of the media has been growing over the past eight years, according to at least four major public opinion surveys. When one such survey, the *Los Angeles Times* poll, recently asked some open-ended questions aimed at learning the reasons for this decline in trust, among the most frequent complaints about journalism was that of "sensationalism in the news."

But sensationalism inevitably follows the release of "revelations." The whole process can be diagrammed: the virtual news assembly line. The newspapers, newscasts, talk shows, and call-ins that are part of the modern media machine pick up on those stories that ninety-nine out of one hundred of these same organizations would not touch on their own, in the first instance. The tales are legitimized by sheer repetition and then distributed far beyond the modest means of the original source (even a "major" book like the one on Walt Disney, for example, seldom has a promotion budget of more than $20,000). Delicately, the Big Media machine distances itself from the inconvenient question of truth, instead it figuratively slaps on a label that reads "A new book published this week says . . ." Reproduction gives the story visibility; it becomes part of the common national conversation. The late-night hosts Jay Leno and David Letterman fashion a few topical jokes: maybe Hoover was out on a case, wearing a disguise. Every one laughs knowingly. The doubters are given play, too, but this makes little perceptual difference, especially if the tale spins around a factoid of observable reality: Disney's reputation as a political conservative, the lack of clues when the body of the Lindbergh baby was found; Hoover's uptight mein and lifelong bachelorhood (he *did* spend a lot of time with his G-man associate, Clyde Tolson). Hoover a homosexual? Oh, right; people have been wondering about that for years . . .

It may make little difference when the story is presented almost totally as an unsubstantiated rumor that is being "authoritatively" denied. The sole eyewitness source for J. Edgar Hoover's Plaza orgies was a convicted perjurer who went through a bitter six-year divorce fight without mentioning the episode once, in or out of court, although it supposedly involved her estranged husband as well. In the world of virtual reality, the fine print may be completely ignored. Researchers at the University of Virginia found that readers reflexively tended to have low opinions of *anyone* whose name appeared in a headline together with the word "Mafia," *independent of what the headline actually said*. That is, the public impressions of the experiment's fictional Smith, Jones, and Doe were statistically identical after people read the following three headlines:

SMITH LINKED TO MAFIA
IS JONES LINKED TO MAFIA?
DOE NOT CONNECTED TO MAFIA

These so-called innuendo effects suggest that the modern media audience is not too discerning as it processes information. Worse, though, the experiment really may signify that the audience, far from being naive, cynically assumes that the media machine would not be "probing" Doe unless he was in fact "linked" to the mob. Either way, it is a measure of the current parlous state of the audience-journalist discourse that psychologists can find meaningful work conducting such experiments. Meanwhile, condolences to mafioso Doe, and tough luck, J. Edgar.

Some critics profess not to be too upset about the emergence of virtual news. They argue that rogue elements have always sensationalized stories, and, concomitantly that there always has been a segment of the audience with an appetite for innuendo, the down-and-dirtier the better. All that really is new these days, this argument goes, is the pervasiveness of the modern media; there is neither quality nor quantity control now. Rumors, lies, and malicious invention appear because the TV magazines, talk shows, all-news channels, the fifteen-minute newswheel of radio, checkout-counter sheets, infotainment magazines, desktop publishers, fax letters, and E-mail bulletin boards all now spew out words and pictures at satellite speed. The news machine needs to be fed its product around the clock.

But more than uncontrolled output is involved. The media ranks of the 1990s threaten to slide back down the evolutionary chain. As the story of news is told, the earliest journalism struggled for its place as the reliable alternative to word of mouth. "The written word evolved in part to stop rumor," says Mitchell Stephens, author of the standard text, *A History of News*.[4] "Print was like turning on a light; dragon sightings got farther from London as the print light grew." There were spectacular throwbacks from time to time. The *New York Sun* promoted a life-on-the-moon scoop in the 1830s; in the 1920s, publisher Bernarr MacFadden ordered his staff to fake photographs and stage reenactments in his newspaper, the *Daily Graphic,* known then as the "daily pornographic." But generally the trend was upward, toward respectability and approximate credibility. Mainstream journalism defined itself by applying the test of truth to stories. The best news managers asked, is this really so? There were editors who actually refused to run a story solely because another paper was carrying it.

A decisive break in the evolutionary chain may have come in early 1981, on the eve of the presidential transition from Jimmy Carter to Ronald Reagan. The *Washington Post*'s Diana McClellan reported in her gossip column "The Ear" that "close pals" of the outgoing president's wife were saying that Blair House, where the Reagans were staying, was bugged and that Jimmy and Rosalynn Carter had eavesdropped on the conversations of Nancy Reagan and the president-elect. Carter denounced the report and said he was going to sue the *Post* for libel. The paper apologized and backed off, but not before the *Post* editorial page offered an imaginative defense. The editorial argued that McClellan had written "a truth"—that "a story was circulating." She had not written that the story was true. The *Post,* says Stephen Bates, the lawyer-author who studied the case, was establishing the "principle" that the existence of a rumor itself is newsworthy, a Ur-moment for the modern information business.[5]

The principle has since been institutionalized on the "people pages" of newspapers and magazines and on the tabloid TV shows. Items are framed around the construct, "People are talking about . . ." In the first months of the Clinton administration alone, "people-are-talking-about"-style rumors involving Donna Shalala, the secretary of the Department of Health and Human Services, and Janet Reno, the U.S. Attorney General, as well as Bill Clinton himself, worked their way into mainstream print. In 1989, it seems, when Shalala was chancellor of the University of Wisconsin, she tangled with student groups about ROTC's presence on campus. At the time, anti-ROTC activists denounced her as a closet lesbian, but offered no evidence for her alleged homosexuality. During an interview on the occasion of Shalala's appointment, the Madison, Wisconsin, *Capital Times* asked about the lesbian story. Shalala denied it. The Associated Press picked up the story on its wires for December 31, 1993: "Clinton Appointee Denies She's a Lesbian."

The Reno story took a slightly different twist. In early March 1993, *Roll Call,* a weekly newspaper that covers the Congress, reported that a National Rifle Association (NRA) lobbyist was spreading "unsubstantiated stories" that Reno had been stopped several times on suspicion of drunk driving. *Roll Call* stressed that the lobbyist tried but could not get Republican lawmakers to move the rumor along. Nevertheless, the NRA angle leveraged the story onto the AP wire; "Rumor on Reno Criticized" read the headline over a New York *Newsday* story that highlighted the drunk driving rumor in its first paragraph. Embarrassed, the NRA fired the lobbyist.

The White House itself came under seige by innuendo. An item in *Newsweek* magazine's "Periscope" section in its April 18, 1993, issue reported rumors of shouting matches between Bill and Hillary Clinton in their private quarters; supposedly she threw a lamp or a book at him. The story was attributed to Secret Service "sources" and took care to point out that some agents had been unhappy with the Clintons, and may have been engaged in a kind of payback. The University of Virginia researchers had a perfect experiment-in-waiting: a poll to determine how many citizens believe that Attorney General Reno drives while drunk and that Hillary Rodham Clinton is a shrewish wife.

A year later, Washington rumormongering was put on a steady, businesslike basis. The conservative political consultant Floyd Brown, through his political action group, Citizens United, established a clearinghouse for dirt about the Clintons. Among other activities, Brown and his associates collected all of the legal documents, stock records, and banking data available on the subject of the Whitewater Development Corporation. Brown also established a kind of sewer catch-basin for tips about the Clintons from around the country, the nastier the rumors the better. His notoriety insured that his E-mail and post office box would be full: he was the producer of the infamous Willie Horton ad in 1988 and the Gennifer Flowers tapes (call 1-900 to hear Flowers and Clinton make pillow talk). More recently, he was heard on his call-in radio show, *Talk Back to Washington*. The materials gathered by Citizens

United were sifted, organized, given a conservative Brownian gloss, and finally offered to reporters from the mainstream news organizations. Brown did not charge for his services. Instead, he counted on the contributions of conservatives reached by his periodic direct-mail solicitations. Brown's tax returns disclosed that he raised $2.2 million in 1992, before the Clintons came to the White House. His retail-rumor business continued to grow in the next fiscal year.

The mainstream journalists who picked up materials from Citizens United "run their own checks and verifications," the *New York Times* rather optimistically explained in its story about Floyd Brown ("A Clinton Nemesis Revels in the Role"). Perhaps, but most journalists of a certain age sense that they and their audience have entered the new territory of Virtual America. The old rules they grew up with have changed and familiar markers moved, as if in the middle of the night, and not just by smarmy publishers, headline writers, gossip columnists, and ideological hit men. When producers for the NBC News magazine show *Dateline* faked a "fiery" car crash and were caught, honest broadcasters like Tom Brokaw resolutely looked on the bright side of the news. The *Dateline* episode, they suggested, could serve as a warning shot, alerting all to "the need for vigilance."

But the really bad news may be that, blurred as the lines seem to be now, the advance of new-media technologies over the next few years promises the final meltdown of standards across the board. The arrival of fiber-optic cameras the size of a hat pin means that video journalists will be able to look through keyholes, literally. "With our old lights and equipment, people saw us coming," says Av Westin, the former ABC newsman and in recent years a senior vice president for Time Warner cable operations. "With a hatcam, you can go anywhere unnoticed. Think what that does to the idea of privacy."

First, reality, then, privacy, and next . . .? Computer techniques now make it possible to recreate photographic images, for example, showing snow in a desert to sell thirst-quenching beer in television commercials. The image-rearrangers quickly moved on to more manipulative projects, such as moving two figures closer together for a "better" picture. Some of these applications were relatively benign; the computer joining of separate photographic images of the two 1994 Olympic skaters, Nancy Kerrigan and Tonya Harding, to make it appear as if they were competing side by side, did no one irreparable harm. Other computer enhancements promise more compromising groupings, say, the head of a public official moved closer to the lips of a second figure, not the official's spouse. "Seeing may be no longer believing," concludes Mitchell Stephens.

The advocates of vigilance, determined as they may be, cannot police the present media system. How will they fare in the next millennium, in the new universe of 100 channels, hatcams and talk shows, Floyd Browns, and cyberflamers?

The Artifice of Politics

Kathleen Hessert leaned forward, carefully studying the flickering image on the video monitor next to her desk. Quickly, she pressed the remote control in her hand to freeze one frame. She jotted on her clipboard, "severe eye dart." The fortysomething man on the monitor was moving his eyes from side to side as he spoke, giving him a shifty look. He also thrust his chin forward every few seconds, a mannerism that had the effect of reinforcing a sense of his nervousness. Hessert scribbled away on her pad, judging the mouth "taut" and the eyes "bulging." But she also noted some positives in the performance; overall, the video image was fixable. Later, Hessert wrote up a list of recommendations to give to her client, the man on the video. "You need to look at someone and hold eye contact for three to five seconds," she suggested. "Your smile is wonderfully warm and attractive. Use it more often, especially at the start and end of interviews and speeches."

The client on the monitor and the woman with the clipboard are both children of our times, and our technology. His job is to be spokesman for a midsized American corporation, manufacturers of a product that . . . well, to be euphemistic about it, as Hessert might advise . . . "occasionally impacts on the environment." His work means he has to meet the press from time to time and appear on television interviews to put his company's side of the story in the best possible light. Her job is to advise people in his situation, to help adjust the light and the sound, so to speak. She is a media consultant, or less delicately, a handler. Handlers make their living telling other people how to behave in front of a television camera, explaining a postmodern version of communications to those who need to promote some message or image. The advice Hessert and others like her give, as we will see, often has little to do with the substance of the spokesperson's remarks; content may count for less than appearance. The aim is not to communicate facts, but an image. This is television, after all, a relatively information-poor but emotionally rich medium.

Hessert's line of work did not exist formally one or two generations ago.[1] The old public relations advisers operated by seat-of-the-pants instincts; there was no pretense of clipboard science or codified behavior. In the 1950s, President Dwight D. Eisenhower made the first concession to the new TV medium, informally engaging the services of the film star Robert Montgomery. Those casual days are over; today, the handlers take themselves very seriously, as do their clients. The handlers' handiwork can be seen all around the television dial, especially at election time. Among the handlers' clients are the sitting president of the United States, U.S. senators and representatives, mayors, and governors—and the candidates who would like to replace them. During the 1992 presidential campaign, the filmmakers D. A. Pennebaker and Chris Hegedus were given access to the "war room," a suite of offices inside Governor Clinton's headquarters in Little Rock, Arkansas, where the candidate's media strategy was plotted. *War Room,* the documentary film that resulted from their work, vividly demonstrated the warrior state of mind of modern campaigns; it also revealed, without commentary, the amoral and ultimately apolitical attitude of approaching political communications solely as a battle of images, waged through mass media. The documentary focused on Bill Clinton's two chief handlers, George Stephanopoulos and James Carville. The candidate himself is seen for less than thirty seconds in the ninety-six-minute film. Stephanopoulos and Carville are present in nearly every frame.[2]

Usually, the handlers are more discreet about their work: the public seldom sees either the strings, or the string-pullers. But the warriors, and their war-room psychology, flourish throughout American political, corporate, and private life. The winsome U.S. Olympic figure skater Nancy Kerrigan had a media adviser, along with a coach, a psychologist-trainer, and a bodyguard (as did the anti-Kerrigan, Tonya Harding). The chairmen of Fortune 500 companies receive instructions on how to talk to the media; so do the contestants who aspire to be Miss America. Handlers exist to help any client with something to promote on television, whether the sales objective is the election of the next leader of the free world or an increased market share of a diet supplement to take unwanted pounds off thighs. As more cable channels appear, and with them, the demand for more political and commercial product, there will be an increase in the demand for handlers' services. The skills they bring to their work will also increase; the best handlers now have their own handlers—public-opinion specialists adept at conducting tracking polls and focus groups—to plumb what consumers think they want and then advise the consultants of these yearnings. This information, in turn, shapes the handlers' recommendations.

All of the handlers' manipulations are intended to be subliminal. The skeptical consumer, with modest help, can learn how to detect the handlers' telltale fingerprints. Forewarned, forearmed.

First of all, the consumer needs to understand how the handlers try to deny their own existence. The word "handler" is too direct and blunt. They prefer to be known by their virtual titles: communications specialist, public relations consultant, or media facilitator, to get away from the implication that they decisively shape the messenger as well as the message being communicated. "We don't hide the candidate, or tint him or try to change him at all," claims

Don Walter, director of research at Ailes Communications, Inc., a handlers' firm whose media credits included the television advertising campaign for George Bush in 1988. But in their promotional efforts to win potential clients, handlers boast of one smashing makeover success after another. Roger Ailes, for example, has never denied the news stories crediting him with a major resculpting of George Bush in the summer of 1988. Ailes coached candidate Bush to lower his voice, rid himself of choppy hand movements, and, in general, eliminate his old money-Yale mannerisms. Ailes made the candidate TV-wise, or wise enough to get elected. Ailes also is known as the author of Ailes' first law of the handlers' code: viewers' opinions of the face on the screen are determined in the first seven seconds of exposure.

Second, no one should be surprised by the variety of clients who think they need to hire a handler. Kathleen Hessert has achieved her successes with business executives—the man suffering from severe eye dart—as well as with winners of the Miss America beauty pageant. Her company, Communications Concepts, Inc., is not a household name; the names of her makeovers are. As a test of the communicator's edge that Communications Concepts provides its clients, Hessert suggests that doubters "watch Miss America at the beginning of her reign and at the end," and compare the two contrasting images. Hessert is a former TV newscaster who worked in midsize markets in New York state before starting her company. She is herself a testimonial to the handlers' skills. In her first jobs on television, Hessert remembers, "I spoke with a strong New Jersey accent, which I didn't even know I had." Through conscious effort, she learned instead to speak in "a more neutral voice."

Andrea Kirby, like Hessert, a former television news reporter, started the Sports Media Workshop in the 1980s. Her clients included the Minnesota Twins baseball team (the year they won the world championship); the National Hockey League's New Jersey Devils; and the Ladies Professional Golf Association's touring members. Kirby can take credit for turning the irascible, press-hating

Twins manager Tom Kelly into "the really sweet wonderful man he is." Basically, Kirby says, she coached Kelly "to accept the fact" that the sports writers who bothered him so much were not as knowledgeable about baseball as he was.

In the 1970s, the influence of the media handlers was confined mostly to political campaigns; by the 1980s, handlers were adding scores of new clients from the business world, especially among the sales forces where presentation is so paramount (in the 1990s, H. Ross Perot became the perfect avatar: the demon salesman morphed into populist champion).

Typically, the corporate training sessions are built around specific cases. In one practice scenario, there has been a recall of a company's product because of an alleged manufacturing defect, or there has been a "toxic event" at one of its plants. The media barbarians are at the gates, demanding information. What do you tell them? Company officials take turns playing the part of hunters and quarry, questioners and spokespersons. After three or four mock news conferences are staged and then critiqued, the company has at least one person prepared to go on camera and face CNN et al. Until the last few years, the handlers and the officials were predominantly, if not exclusively, male. These days, women have moved toward stage center, both as handlers and as spokespersons.

Whether they are male or female, coaching presidential candidates or professional athletes, the handlers usually dispense much the same advice, while charging fees as high as the market will bear. The services of a political consulting firm of the stature of Ailes Communications can run as high as $25,000 a month during a year-long campaign, plus a percentage of all TV time purchased for the candidates' advertising (such commissions can add up to six or seven figures). The handlers move easily back and forth among disparate clients. The Sawyer/Miller Group in New York worked on the political campaigns of Ohio Senator John Glenn and Philippine President Corazon Aquino; in the mid-1980s, David Sawyer counseled Nancy Reagan to help her repair some of the damage done by Kitty Kelley's unauthorized biography. In the same period, one of Sawyer's associates, John Scanlon, buffed the images of such diverse clients as the Mobil Oil Company, the television newsman Peter Jennings, and Ivana Trump, the former wife of the New York real estate developer.

Scanlon was extremely well connected; his most effective work on behalf of his clients was often done one on one, sometimes by telephone. Other handlers employed more formal methods. Hessert, for example, developed an elaborate handbook, the "Media Relations Playbook," and an accompanying audio-cassette tape for the players of the National Football League (NFL). The NFL hired Hessert after a late 1980s public relations disaster (a New England Patriots player supposedly exposed himself in the presence of a *Boston Herald* sportswriter named Lisa Olsen). Hessert's "Playbook" offered tips to players on how to conduct a good interview; it noted that the chances for endorsement contracts rise with polished verbal skills pre- and postgame, as well as with a good performance on the field. Appearances are stressed: dress nicely, don't sit with your legs spread wide apart ("it's not an attractive camera shot"), don't slouch, and, of course, watch those darty eyes. "Never look down when you answer," the "Playbook" instructed. "It makes you look guilty." In case the athlete forgets the "Playbook" points, Hessert provided a reminder in the form of a small plastic card that can be held in the palm of a hand during the on-camera interview. The advice included the terse admonitions "be yourself," "be precise," "don't be baited," and "don't forget you're always on." As with Miss America, the home viewer could judge who has benefited from media coaching, and how good a student he or she was.

Some of the handlers' advice is self-evident. Mothers have been telling their children to sit up straight ever since there were chairs. Amazingly, though, many otherwise accomplished people cannot think in any clear-eyed way when the television camera's red light goes on. Robert Bork was probably one of the smartest judicial minds ever to be turned down as a U.S. Supreme Court justice. When the Bork confirmation hearings began in September 1987, he did it his way, alone. He sat by himself at a small table in the hearing room. His family was on hand, but not placed in a location where they would show up in the TV camera angles. When Bork was pressed by hostile questioners, he acted beleaguered and overly defensive. In the television coverage, he appeared isolated—a visual cue to his opponents' claim that he was outside the American mainstream. And, as one Washington handler told us, "his pointy beard didn't help, either."

Perhaps nothing would have helped Bork, given the ideological nature of his opposition. But things were different in the same Senate hearing room for the confirmation of a proposed U.S. Supreme Court justice, just four years later. The Clarence Thomas hearings became a handlers' heaven. Nothing was left to chance by the specialists working on Thomas's behalf. Weeks before the hearings, a team of Bush White House aides was given responsibility to get the Thomas nomination through. The aides worked under the direction of Kenneth M. Duberstein, the former Reagan adviser who went on to become a private consultant and major Washington rainmaker. Team members used tape measures to figure camera angles. They checked the lighting and the size and placement of the witness table. Thomas underwent grilling in mock sessions. By the time his confrontation with Anita Hill began, Thomas was prepared. When the hearings commenced, Thomas's wife, Virginia, was seated so that she would be in the frame of the close-up shots as Thomas testified: the supportive wife, standing by her man in the face of sexual harassment charges. Thomas's main Senate sponsor, John Danforth of Missouri, also was seated to be in the same frame. Handlers helped with Thomas's responses, including his fiery, antihandler statement—when he portrayed himself, falsely, as his own speechwriter. The scripted presentation was credited with helping turn around public opinion on his nomination.

Viewers should be warned that the handlers' hand extends far beyond hearing tables and courtrooms. When William Kennedy Smith first appeared on the nation's screens, he seemed like a public relations nightmare: a loutish-looking young man accused of rape. Just before his trial began in Palm Beach, he could be seen romping on the Florida beach with a black labrador puppy, named McShane. Cameras promptly recorded the sight. Later, the *New York Daily News* sourly suggested it was a handler's restaging of an old scene starring his uncle, John F. Kennedy. Was it an attempt to present Camelot Revisited? The handlers handled that, too. Barbara Gamarekian, a former *New York Times* reporter, was brought in by the Kennedy-Smith family to act as the "media liaison person" for Smith. She demurred at the suggestion of staging: "Most families with kids have dogs and if you have a home on the oceanfront you obviously run on the beach."

Children are the handlers' favored (two-legged) prop, as well. David Duke, a former member of the Ku Klux Klan, ran for governor of Louisiana a few years ago. The KKK's ideology may be racist and backward looking, but Duke's candidacy was quite up to date. Although Duke was divorced, he gained "media custody" of his two blond-haired children for the duration of the campaign. They appeared with him at rallies, photo opportunities, and TV interviews. According to Jerry Hagstrom, then covering the political-consultants' business for the *National Journal* in Washington, the handlers always advise the candidate to appear with children or dogs, "even when they don't have any."

They also advise their clients to *avoid* certain props. During the Whitewater Development Corporation investigations in the spring of 1994, Clinton senior counselor George Stephanopoulos was summoned to testify before a grand jury in Washington. A group of reporters and photographers waited for him to emerge from the D.C. Courts building. Knowing that they would be there, Stephanopoulos took care to handle his own image carefully. He made a big point of flagging a taxicab in the street to return to the White House: just another Washingtonian going to work. By the next morning, however, he had returned to his normal mode of transportation around town—his chauffeur-driven limousine from the White House motor pool.

The major religious institutions of the world have existed for centuries; a few have existed for millennia. Some of the biggest have resolved not to be left behind in the interactive age. The department of communications of the National Council of Churches in New York City does more than help promulgate the Word of God to Protestant ministers and their congregants. For church members likely to deal with the media, the department provides help in the form of a thirteen-point checklist entitled "how to provide a good interview to print or electronic journalists." In San Francisco, Father Miles Riley conducts media training workshops for Roman Catholic Church leaders, advising bishops on the best ways to deal with television interviewers. Father Riley told us he has a dream. "I want to conduct a media workshop for Pope John Paul," he said. "The Holy Father is a fabulous communicator. But I want to get those microphones out of his face and put his script on a teleprompter." Sometimes, even God's Shepherd needs guidance.

The handlers' skills stir unsettling thoughts about where the layers of handling end and the "real thing" begins. Is there a there *there* under the cosmeticized surface of the media handlers' work? In his first year in office, Bill Clinton clearly was at ease on camera; he projected intelligence and warmth. Sometimes he seemed to be presiding at a permanent town meeting. He was attractive and well spoken; he looked good on TV. At the same time, he seemed curiously vague on certain matters of substance, particularly those involving foreign policy. One critic, Leon Weiseltier, observed that often Clinton "seems to think that he has acted when he has merely spoken."[3] While the impression grew that Clinton was perhaps more talk-show host than chief executive, no one argued that his presidency was not entertaining.

But if communications skills are so important in the interactive age, then why not go all the way and recruit political leaders from the ranks of entertainers? The career of Ronald Reagan represents an early, tentative test-run of the notion. Although Reagan was assuredly an Hollywood actor, he did not go immediately into politics. Rather, he spent almost a decade in the transitional role of media spokesman for the General Electric company, acting as part of the handlers' brigade. Only then did he run for governor of California. A more recent, though jokey, example of politics as entertainment was provided by the spectacle of radio talk-show host Howard Stern's short-lived candidacy for governor of New York on the Libertarian Party ticket. Stern had won celebrity in the early 1990s on morning drive time; his radio program featured boy's locker-room humor, in particular an adolescent's fascination with male and female private parts. He became a best-selling author and host of a New Year's Eve television program offered nationally on pay-per-view cable channels. In the spring of 1994, Stern incorporated his genital humor into a bid for the Libertarian nomination, showing up at the party's convention with an entourage of decolletaged women. He campaigned for a time on the air, and confounded critics who dismissed him as just another dirty-talker by adding a chilling edge to his candidacy; if elected, he said, he would bring back the death penalty to New York.[4]

The Libertarians usually were described as a fringe party or splinter group, and Stern was depicted as just one more show-business sharpie adept at milking the media for publicity. In short, he was his own best handler. But the national Republican Party, the Grand Old Party of Lincoln and Eisenhower, was not immune from talk-show fever, either. In Bill Clinton, the rival Democrats had a president who was comfortable at the microphone: a politician who gave good media. While Clinton excelled in his national talk-show duties in the first three years of his presidency, Republicans fretted that their party of opposition was unable to muster a comparable host from its traditional ranks. Senior congressional Republicans, such as Bob Dole and Alphonse D'Amato, fell short of filling the role. So did such 1996 Republican presidential hopefuls as Texas Senator Phil Gramm, Lamar Alexander, and Governor Pete Wilson of California. Some failed to win the talk-host part for reasons of age, or looks, or personality tics; others were judged unsuitable because they were too hot for the cool TV medium. House Speaker Newt Gingrich had energy and intelligence, but ran the risk of becoming a pain in the ear—overexposed, harsh, ultra-hot. Only the Tennessean, Lamar Alexander, a former Bush administration cabinet officer, systematically used the new technologies for his 1996 presidential bid. Throughout 1995, Alexander materialized as a public Mr. High Tech, mobilizing support via a monthly "Republican Neighborhood Meeting," an earnest one-hour presentation beamed by satellite to 500 local cable systems; later he added a site on the World Wide Web. The real Alexander campaign developed off camera, as his fundraisers collected the millions needed to keep the Alexander show on the road (estimated cost *per day,* according to the *New York Times:* $70,000).

In this situation, the media personality Rush Limbaugh emerged as the most consistent conservative performer of the mid-1990s. Like Howard Stern, Limbaugh was a full-time professional entertainer. Unlike Stern, Limbaugh's supporting cast included the veteran master-handler Roger Ailes, a force worth far more in the marketing of the star than Stern's bevy of undressed women.

Limbaugh was an entertainer who happened to be a conservative Republican. The sequence is important; his entrepreneur's interests drove his political ideology. That made him a model representative of the interactive age. With the Clintons in the White House, Limbaugh's business prospects soared: it was a good time to run against Washington. On his radio call-in show, carried by his Excellence in Broadcasting network, Limbaugh ceaselessly ragged on Clinton while promoting the Limbaugh oeuvre, including his autobiography, *The Way Things Ought To Be,* not once, but a half dozen times per hour. If he liked a particular caller's comments, say, a "joke" about Hillary Rodham Clinton's trades in cattle futures, Limbaugh sent the caller an autographed copy of his latest book. These were virtual texts; typically, they consisted of the commentator's radio monologues, recycled for print. Limbaugh also managed to mention one or another of his paid personal appearances, as well as plug his advertisers ("I just used Compu-Serve to call up information on the Democrats' family leave bill . . .") On the seventh day, he did not rest. On the commercial breaks of his radio show, a prerecorded Limbaugh touted hair-growing products.[5]

Limbaugh's foray into late-night television began in 187 television markets in the last year of the Bush administration. By the second year of the Clinton administration the show was being syndicated to 250 stations covering 99 percent of the country. The show was pure Rush: no guests, no audience participation, no announcer-foil, no backup band, with time only for one or two viewer calls. Instead, viewers heard show-biz shtick for twenty-two minutes—a half hour minus the eight precious minutes for commercials. The Limbaugh show was talk radio on TV; it featured the host's signature riffs aimed at feminists, environmentalists, liberals, and other enemies of the Republic. Roger Ailes was listed as the show's executive producer and one of its co-owners: Bush '88, Rush '92; presidential campaign, late-night talk. Ailes moved easily from one to the other.

Critics observed Limbaugh and Ailes together and saw a partnership of two lookalike, soundalike ideologues. Both came out of the American heartland, Limbaugh from Cape Girardeau, Missouri, Ailes from Warren, Ohio. Appearances can be deceptive. Both men were extremely smart, sophisticated, and focused. The precept of the conservative credo they embraced most vigorously was that of free private enterprise. They both enjoyed the rewards of business success.

Limbaugh, born in 1951, earned $2 million a year in the first years of the Clinton administration, thanks to the market value of opposition (during the months the Whitewater investigation dragged on, Limbaugh's late-night TV ratings approached those of the pure entertainment programs on competing channels). Ailes was ten years older than Limbaugh; his earnings put him in the same top tax bracket. Post-Bush and Reagan, Ailes counseled such corporate clients as General Electric, AT & T, and the American Bankers Association. Both men lived in New York City and revel in the cultural elite's good life as much as any liberal. Limbaugh had moved east from a Sacramento talk show in 1988, concluding that New York was the place to launch a national show (many of the advertising agencies that buy the commercial time on radio and TV were in Manhattan). Limbaugh, the broadcast host, attacked New York and its liberal politics on the air while Limbaugh, the bon vivant, praised the city's restaurants and elite-class services ("I love having things delivered to the door," he wrote in his autobiography). Indeed, Limbaugh and Ailes first met at "21," a premiere expense-account restaurant, where they were both regulars. "He liked me and I liked him," Ailes told us. "The deal came later, after the friendship."

Ailes's role in the Rush Limbaugh Show was similar to his work for former clients Reagan and Bush or for any of the U.S. senators he helped get elected or reelected. "I hired the staff and put the tv elements together," Ailes said. Ailes also helped bring in the third partner, Multimedia Entertainment, producers and distributors of *Donahue*, as well as owners of a newspaper chain, television and radio stations, and cable franchises. In a way, Ailes never left show business. He was a brash producer for the *Mike Douglas Show* when Richard Nixon was booked as a guest. The year was 1967, and the former vice president was between jobs. But he made note of Ailes's confident prediction that no one would ever be elected president again without a presentable television manner. Ailes later went to work for the Nixon campaign in 1968, and then settled in New York and returned to entertainment, producing the off-Broadway hit, "Hot L Baltimore." He did a brisk business moving back and forth between electoral politics and popular entertainment in the 1970s and 1980s, producing prime-time television specials for Steve Allen, and making TV spots for the Reagan and Bush campaigns.

While entrepreneur Ailes quickly gained clients and fame, Limbaugh required more time to establish his particular brand-name identity. First in Sacramento and then in New York, he gradually shaped his monologues to follow a Reaganesque gospel: limited government, family values, peace through strength, "growth" over "apocalyptic environmentalism," prayer in public schools, recognition of the "fundamental differences between men and women." He told us that he really believes what he says on the air—his family has voted Republican for 100 years—but added, with refreshing honesty, "I am first a broadcaster." The radio program and the syndicated television show are for-profit enterprises, "not some boring public service forum." Radio and TV, he explains, "are total show biz. So many things go on that you've got to cut through the noise. With a thousand conservative commentators talking, my bombast and humor is a way to stand out. The reaction is, 'My gosh, I didn't know there's a funny conservative out there.'"

The humor is part of the counterprogramming, one of the bedrock principles of multichannel media. Counterprogramming requires a talent or show to be consistent, to find its niche, and then play to that audience with a distinctive look and sound. On television, the constant anti-Clinton ideology underlying Limbaugh's show-business style helped distinguish him from the other mainstream television-programming choices. The late-night hosts Jay Leno and David Letterman, for example, had fun at the expense of conservatives as well as liberals. But even with Limbaugh, the political never overwhelmed the personal. While the silent majority determines the election every four years, Limbaugh says, "my own success is determined not by who wins the presidency but by the size of my audience."

The Limbaugh audience was hardly a majority; neither was it the stereotypical silent conservative legion. An estimated 2.5 million listeners tuned to his radio show on a typical day in 1994. Men outnumbered women three to one. The bulk of the audience was in the twenty-one to forty-nine age bracket, markedly different from the gerontocracy tuned to conservative commentators from an earlier era, like Paul Harvey. These younger viewers worked in white-collar jobs and believed in the power of self-improvement, or so the advertising time-buyers thought; among Limbaugh advertisers were Hooked on Phonics and Speed Spanish, along with Subaru and the National Rifle Association. These were post–civil rights era, post–women's movement men, and Limbaugh gave them Reaganism with a rock-and-roll beat. A resident company of actors offered taped playlets between Limbaugh monologues. The Andy Williams version of the wildlife anthem "Born Free" was punctuated with machine gun fire and mortar explosions (gotcha!, animal rights wackos). Dion's "The Wanderer" (circa 1960s) was retitled "The Philanderer" and sung by a Senator Edward Kennedy impersonator ("'Cause I'm a Kennedy, yes I'm Ted Kennedy/ I sleep around, around, around, around . . ."). Hillary Clinton was ridiculed in a mock trailer for the motion picture "Single White Female . . . the terror coming to your neighborhood soon." SWF has a dog named Willie. "Hillary" orders: "Now, Sit." Sound of panting dog. Then: "You made a cabinet appointment without asking me? Who's in charge around here?"

Some of this comic-book dialog has been done before, by the Spike Jones orchestra or the skit writers of *Saturday Night Live*. Similarly, Limbaugh's 1990s' "feminist jokes" might have come from the 1960s' black-and-white TV shows of Groucho Marx ("I like the women's movement, from behind"). But single white males in the audience could not seem to get enough of the conservative laugh lines; Limbaugh's radio network went from 50 stations to over 500 in four years. *Limbaugh,* the TV show, used the same locker-room material. In the first show, Limbaugh put on his newscaster's this-just-in look and reported that the public schools of Los Angeles had adopted a new safe-sex curriculum. The program is called Outercourse. One of the subjects: Masturbation 101. Hoo-heee![6]

Ailes watching on a monitor, smiled broadly. The Limbaugh style, he said, works better on television than radio: "he's visual, he's emotional, he's good tv." Ailes added: "We let Rush be Rush. He's a star. I couldn't change him if I tried. I want them to unthink all they thought they knew about tv. Let this sucker roll. Improvisational tv." A number of critics pointed out that Limbaugh's improvisations on both his TV and radio shows were often at the expense of truth.[7] The environmentalists' case for global warming is dismissed by grade-school logic: a video compilation of winter blizzards. When "good looking studs" are on trial, women should not be on juries because they voted to acquit the Menendez brothers (in fact only one brother was acquitted). Limbaugh reported that the "liberal" Sidwell Friends school, where Chelsea Clinton was a student, assigned eighth graders to write a paper on "Why I feel guilty being white." The school denied the story unequivocally; it also pointed out that its student body was one-quarter nonwhite.

None of this slowed Limbaugh. On camera, he smiled and bid the audience good night: "The critics say we won't last but I'm not going off the air until I convince everyone in America that I'm right." He was being funny, of course.

Voice of the People:
Loud and Unclear

8

Journalists are always on the alert to find a "defining moment"—an episode or event that seems to reveal some wider truth about politics or politicians. One such moment occurred early in the first year of the Clinton administration, when the new president flew on Air Force One to Michigan, and then went by motorcade to a television studio in Southfield, outside Detroit, for one of his electronic town meetings. The Southfield event was an ETM-squared. While the president appeared on the screen, a group of carefully selected American citizens hundreds of miles away watched around a table, each man and woman equipped with a small electronic box connected to a computer. This was a dial group, called together by the public opinion specialist Stanley B. Greenberg, a former academic now known in Washington as "the president's pollster." As Clinton answered questions on the TV monitor, members of the dial group, recruited for their demographic profile and paid for their efforts, worked the controls on their handheld boxes to register their positive or negative reactions to the words and images on the screen. Their dial scale gave them a reaction range of 0 to 100. Moment by moment, all of these individual responses were fed into the computer; a special software program added up the "score" to trace a continuous approval-dis-approval line on the computer screen that Greenberg's associates were monitoring.

Greenberg's dial group was an electronic, interactive variant of that standard tool of market research, the focus group (FG). Dial groups are to focus groups what E-mail is to "snailmail" (standard letters). In FGs, citizens' reactions are elicited in question-and-answer sessions led by a skilled practitioner. Such sessions usually last around two hours; typically, they are tape recorded and observed by other experts through a one-way viewing glass. Sometimes the market researchers disclose the client for whom they are working. Other times the product—sitting president or new soft drink—is kept vague. Participants receive $35 to $50 for their time, although on occasion FG experts interview other (so-called) experts in more intense one-on-one sessions. Not too long ago one of our group was interviewed by a New York market research firm; the purpose was kept unspecified, except to say that the researchers were acting on behalf of AT & T, "a client interested in communications."[1]

If the Greenbergian dial group episode had ended there, with Clinton in Southfield, it would have been "defining" enough: the president's chief public opinion specialist had his record of the group's gut reactions to Clinton, the better to help the White House understand public opinion—or, in the extreme, to help it make public policy. But there was an added bonus for the journalistic snoop, a satori of Zen revelation. While Clinton spoke and Greenberg monitored the twists and turns of his audience, another dial group was meeting in a similar setting. This second FG was arranged by Frederick T. Steeper, a Republican public opinion analyst who had done dial groups for the George Bush White House. Steeper invited reporters to his session to publicize the political uses of the dial-group art. It was an offer that could not be refused.[2]

Every White House staff since the 1960s has made full-time use of the opinion sampler's skills. John Kennedy engaged a young specialist named Louis Harris to conduct public opinion polls. The Nixon administration kept asking, worriedly, how its policies were "playing in Peoria" (that is, in Middle America).[3] In 1988, Vice President Bush's campaign themes of flag, family, and furloughs (the Willie Horton fable) emerged from focus-group research. Most recently, the Clinton presidency has been especially attuned to its volatile constituencies of moderate and lapsed Democrats, younger suburbanites and self-proclaimed independents in the Peorias of the nation. Before the 1992 presidential primaries, Clinton advisers Mandy Grunwald and Frank Greer determined through focus groups and polls that the public was increasingly unhappy with "media politics"—the sound bites, staged events, and attack advertising of the modern political campaign. According to Greer, the voting classes were ready for someone very much like the wonkish Clinton, with his devotion to "the issues." Consequently, as we saw, when the campaign press got so hot and bothered by Gennifer Flowers during the New Hampshire primaries, Grunwald and Greer bought airtime on the state's commercial stations for a Clinton-led ETM stressing the economy and jobs; they followed that performance by booking the candidate on television the next night for a program of unscreened phone calls, in the manner of C-SPAN.

Clinton did like to talk at great length about public policy, and the New Hampshire strategy presumably reflected the man. It is only fair to point out, however, that his polls were suggesting there was nothing else he could do. His best hope, the sole alternative he and his staff had available to them, was to change the subject. The press wanted to talk about "the character issue," while "the economy" was a topic on the minds of many New Hampshire voters, as scoped out by the public opinion surveyors. Clinton followed what the polls told him, and did well by being a good populist.

Far from breaking with the past practices of calculated "media campaigning," the 1990s' candidates and their interactive tech-

niques for tapping into populist angst may have achieved the ultimate media manipulation: the ability to find out what the various
publics want, in particular, those key demographic groups that are
needed on election day, and then giving it to them. Or, at their
most cynical, the candidates employ the arts of opinion sampling
to determine the desires of core constituencies, and then give the
appearance of meeting their wants.

Some skeptics believe that is how the pulse-taking form is
more or less always used. The public opinion specialist Frank Luntz
told the *Wall Street Journal* in the spring of 1994 that the words
Clinton used in the great health-care debate of 1993–94 "come
right out of Stan Greenberg's focus groups." According to Luntz,
"Greenberg literally pulls the words out of the mouths of ordinary
Americans and puts them in the mouth of president." As a result,
"Bill Clinton speaks like real Americans speak." Offering an example of this "interactive" relationship, the *Journal* cited the president's
speech to Congress on health care in September 1993. Clinton's
speech, it will be recalled, offered six basic principles for reforming
the country's health-care system, namely, "security, simplicity, savings, choice, quality and responsibility." As Luntz explained it, he
was doing focus groups in the months leading up to the president's
speech and "those were the exact words I was hearing."[4]

Luntz is a registered Republican, as well as the pollster who
did work for Newt Gingrich on the Contract with America. His
spin on the Clinton-Greenberg collaboration should be seen in that
light (it is to Clinton's enemies' interest to depict him as a poll-
driven panderer). Still, no one doubts the importance of polling
and other forms of "interactivity" in the Clinton White House.
While Greenberg himself declines to discuss the specifics of what
he tells the president, he confirmed that he met once a week with
Clinton during the first two years of his presidency. In the same
period, too, Greenberg also talked almost every day with presidential counselor George Stephanopoulos and also regularly sent five-
to ten-page memos summarizing the Greenberg research findings

to Vice President Al Gore and to other senior administration officials. As Greenberg told James Barnes of the *National Journal:* "Clinton has a special need to bring the people with him in his presidency. We need popular support to keep the pressure on the Congress to vote for change . . . I view my role as how to keep the people with us through some tough decisions."[5] Because Greenberg is so obviously a very sophisticated operative, his auditors can be forgiven for thinking that the words used by the pollster to describe *his* work also came out of some of his own dial groups. After all, someone who wants us to "vote for change," who makes "very tough decisions," sounds very much like the strong leader the voters say they want. In a word, such a leader is acting *presidential.*

More than sixty years ago, the Marxist critic Walter Benjamin (1892–1940) wrote about works of art in what he called an age of mass reproduction. The audience, Benjamin suggested, was becoming conscious of the process behind the surface of the message. Today, in our era of electronic mass reproduction, we cannot escape our knowledge of these processes; in fact, audience skepticism about the communications art form is essential. While policymakers and the marketers of new products spend money and time conceiving of fresh ways to measure the desires of the voter/consumer, the shortcomings of these same tools of analysis have become more and more apparent. Polling, group-sampling techniques, and interactive research all require a series of warning labels, cautioning users to handle carefully.

For one, focus-group questions typically put a premium on easily grasped ideas. In Miami in the spring of 1994, voters at an FG pulled together by Democratic Party operatives were asked to fill in the following sentence: "I'M FEELING (BLANK) ABOUT BILL CLINTON." The one-word emotional response requested inevitably led to simplistic touchy-feely results; among the words supplied were "stressed," "concerned," and "unhappy." The same group was then asked to sum up its economic expectations for 1995 in the form of a weather forecast; the question produced predictably shallow replies. Respondents suggested "drizzle," "showers," and "cloudy." The researchers got exactly what they deserved: weather reports rather than a sense of climate.

Similarly, Ross Perot's citizens' organization, United We Stand America, held a national television forum in the spring of 1993 that attracted an audience of 20 million. In connection with the TV show, the Perot group designed what it called "The First National Referendum—Government Reform." The referendum featured a "ballot" with seventeen questions, all printed in an advertisement in *TV Guide.* The weekly had a paid circulation of some 15 million at the time the ad appeared and a readership that skewed toward older, nonurban, white Americans, the same ranks that provide the bulk of Perot supporters. Within a month, almost 1.3 million "ballots" were received, tabulated by congressional district, and delivered to Capitol Hill. Questions 6 and 8 were typical of the way the referendum was stacked to produce the desired results:

Question 6: If the government wants the American people to pay more taxes, should it provide leadership by example—all sacrifice begins at the top—by cutting Congress' and the president's salaries by ten percent and reducing their retirement plans to bring them in line with those of the American people?

Question 8: Should Congress and officials in the White House set the example for sacrifice by eliminating all perks and special privileges currently paid by taxpayers?

Unsurprisingly, identical 98.3 percent majorities favored the two proposals. Who is not in for "fairness" and lower taxes? In fact, all seventeen questions resulted in the desired "yes" vote with the yesses never dropping below 93 percent. The wonder is that even a very small, very ornery percentage of the self-selected sample bothered to write in and vote "no."[6]

The public opinion specialists are themselves aware that the way questions are posed to the public can shape the replies. Thus, a sample can be "scientific"—that is, truly random rather than skewed by unbalanced responses—and still produce a predetermined result. Yankelovich Partners, Inc., polling on behalf of *Time* magazine and CNN in May 1994, neatly demonstrated how wording can decisively influence responses. A telephone sample of 600 American adults was asked if the government was spending too much money "on assistance to the poor." Only 23 percent answered "yes." Then a similar random sample was asked if the government was spending too much money "on welfare." This time, the "yes" responses rose to 53 percent.

History and memory themselves can be trampled by bad polling techniques. Not long ago, the American Jewish Committee (AJC) asked Roper Starch Worldwide, a respected polling organization, to examine public attitudes toward Jews. The Roper poll came after some publicity was generated by a couple of "Holocaust deniers"—crackpots who spun theories that the killing of 6 million European Jews by Nazi Germany had been exaggerated, or that the deaths were actually due to cholera and other "natural" causes. In late 1992, Roper published the results of its survey; the figures purported to show that one in every five Americans doubted that the Holocaust had happened: this, despite the photographic and written evidence of the extermination campaign and the eyewitness reports of Americans and others toward the end of World War II— indeed, the entire sweep of history from 1933 to 1945. The results were almost literally unthinkable, shaking many people's confidence in the U.S. educational system and causing anguish among American Jews. The figure showed up in speeches, news stories, and television discussions about the "power" of the Holocaust-denial movement. Thoughtful commentators debated how, in media world, truth itself had been put on the defensive, and the deniers' "position" accorded weight, as one more way of thinking about Jews and Nazis. In a talk-show culture, the columnist John

Leo pointed out in *U.S. News & World Report,* everyone who picks up the phone has equal status, "flat-earthers and round-earthers, Holocaust deniers and Holocaust historians, people who speak regularly to interplanetary aliens and people who don't."[7]

But then a few public opinion specialists went beyond all the hand wringing to take a second look at the data, specifically at the way the Holocaust question had been phrased in the Roper-AJC poll. This was the wording:

Does it seem possible or does it seem impossible to you that the Nazi extermination of the Jews never happened?

About 22 percent of the survey had replied that "it seemed possible" that the Holocaust never happened. As written, the double negative construction was hard enough to grasp when read in its printed form; when heard over the telephone, it was even more confusing. Yet the "finding" was cited as accurate for over a year. Finally, confronted with a Gallup poll that contradicted the 22 percent figure and pressed by critics, Roper publicly acknowledged that the way it had asked the question was flawed. The Anti-Defamation League of the B'nai B'rith (ADL), a leading American Jewish organization devoted to publicizing anti-Semitic acts, made known its second thoughts on the poll. That took some soul searching, too. The work of the ADL and the AJC is directly affected by such numbers. If the denier movement is attracting adherents, both organizations have potent levers to push in the Jewish community, to solicit donations and support for their work.

A new poll was commissioned with the Holocaust question put this way:

Does it seem possible to you that the Nazi extermination of the Jews never happened, or do you feel certain that it did happen?

This time, only 1 percent of the survey said it was possible that the Holocaust never happened.

The story, then, has a happy ending, with the news not nearly as bad as previously thought. Not quite. The polling community and a few other specialists who read the short follow-up articles, deep inside a few elite newspapers, noted the correction. Too often, the follow-up articles never quite catch up to the original sensational stories. The factoid "one-in-five-Americans-doubt-Holocaust-happened" became part of the intellectual junk orbiting the atmosphere. Like the debris of a spent space rocket, it was there, contaminating the air, long after its misbegotten launching.

Public opinion polls solicit opinions that may be loosely held, or not held at all. Rather, they are blurted out under the prodding of the questioner. For that matter, many people regularly contradict themselves in focus groups and public opinion interviews, express-ing warring views one right after another. This cognitive disso-nance—the ability to hold two (or more) views at odds with each other—seems to be part of the human conditions. And so a public opinion sampling can be conducted in a sophisticated manner, the questions carefully presented, the phrasing unambiguous, and the sponsoring client able to rise above its partisan interests and organ-izational needs . . . and still the results can be flawed, their "impli-cations" without real meaning. The health-care debate in the first years of the Clinton presidency stands in as a good case study. According to the public opinion polls, the focus groups and the dial groups, the American public was worried about the health-care system and expressed its desire for "change," "solutions," and "gov-ernment action" (all positive words). But at the same time, the same public said it did not want to increase the size of that same gov-ernment being asked to do something.

The public also showed it was capable of believing demon-strably wrong "facts," past and prospective, about health care. In the summer of 1994, for example, public opinion polls showed that fully two-thirds of the voters thought that the Clinton administra-tion had raised their taxes and that it intended to raise them more with its health-reform package. The former belief was untrue for most tax brackets. The latter belief was equally false, according to the provisions of the Clinton plan. The work of the Congress fared no better. A *Washington Post*-ABC News poll found that many Americans believe the 1994 Congress had passed a major bill limiting immigration (it had not) as believe it had cut the deficit (it had).[8] In the interactive world, everyone is encouraged to sound off; but some people have little of substance to communicate on some subjects. Sadly, too, some citizens understand little of the questions asked them. This does not stay the public opinion analysts from their appointed rounds. In a joke the experts tell on themselves, a pollster asks a citizen: "Do you think Americans are ignorant and apathetic?" The citizen responds: "I don't know and I don't care."

In June 1994, just before the celebration of the Gay Olympic Games in New York City, the *Yankelovich Monitor* released a national study of the consumer habits of gays and lesbians. The *New York Times'* advertising column gave extensive attention to the findings. Marketing specialists called the results eye-opening; the *Monitor's* study was described as an improvement over previous studies, as well as a confirmation of earlier speculations. According to the *Monitor,* gays and lesbians on average were better educated than the national heterosexual population, and more likely to be self-employed and live in major metropolitan areas. Gays and lesbians were said to be more consumption oriented and quicker to adapt to technological change. But a number of skeptics, including Professor Fred Fejes of Florida Atlantic University, pointed out that the survey depended on lesbian and gay respondents to discuss that they were homosexual. This introduced one skewing factor: an educated, urbane, affluent, urban man or woman is, in fact, generally the kind of person who would disclose his or her sexual orientation. Similarly, the finding that gays and lesbians were likely to be more "cutting edge" in their tastes again was a characteristic of educated, urbane, men and women who were in a position to be open about their sexuality. Fejes corrected the record in a letter to the *Times,* pointing out that studies requiring "the respondent to disclose information about sexual orientation tend vastly to underrepresent lesbians and gays who are appreciably older or younger, members of minority groups, residents of rural or conservative parts of the country, or from lower socioeconomic groups." Homosexuals in these categories, he argued, are much less willing to disclose sexual orientation information "for reasons of personal history or fear of discrimination or harassment." Far from being a window on the gay and lesbian community, the "enlightened" *Monitor* study instead helped perpetuate longstanding stereotypes and misinformation to the wider population.

Many of the people who participate in such surveys try to tell the truth, or what appears to them to be the truth (that is, if they respond at all). Small-town, working-class homosexuals are not the only group that may decide to stay closeted; tax delinquents, men behind in their alimony payments, deadbeat fathers, members of the underground economy, among others, may choose to be uncounted for any number of personal reasons. On the other hand, a number of people see the great national love affair with political polls and market research as an opportunity to influence the system rather than inform it. They seek out the survey researchers' questionnaire forms and microphones. The 1-900 number poll idea is the latest form of pseudo-science. CBS News asked viewers to phone in their "votes" on a talk-back feature on the program *America Tonight.*[9] A kudzu growth of opinion purveyors has sprung up in the fertile soil of the interactive age. On many talk shows, the hosts have gotten to know "Charlie from Spring Valley," "Phil the sales rep," and other regulars. The 1990 edition of the *Guinness Book of World Records* awarded the distinction of most-letters-to-the-editor-published to Walt Seifert, a professor emeritus of journalism at Ohio State University and a longtime member of the advisory board of the right-wing group, Accuracy in Media (AIM). Guinness credited Seifert with 1,600 letters published; in 1993, Seifert, then in his eighties, advised his AIM colleagues that he had raised his record to over 2,000. Trying to be helpful to fellow conservatives who wanted to protest easternliberalmediabias—pronounced as one word among the believers—the AIM group published a handbook of advice, "How to Write Letters to the Media."[10]

AIM founder Reed Irvine also promoted the interactive ideas of Mort Rosenblum, a longtime Associated Press reporter based in Paris. In his book, *Who Stole the News?*, Rosenblum suggested that four to six letters a week from "concerned" (read, conservative) readers, addressed to an executive or a managing editor, were sufficient "to influence the mix in news columns." Rosenblum advised writers to send their letters to a specific editor, whose name can be found on the masthead of a newspaper or magazine. "'Personal' on the envelope helps move it along." Television station managers and network executives "are used to numbers, percentages, focus group reports," and so individual communications "cannot help but make an impact." Although television executives are harder to reach than newspaper editors, the effort is worthwhile because "each of them lives and dies on the ability to read the public mood." Rosenblum then offered readers of the "AIM Report" some informal tips, including the commonsense advice that, "if you get mad enough to cancel a subscription, go directly to the editor." An irate call to a bored and overworked circulation clerk makes no impact. He likened such a call to complaining and walking out on a French waiter, "who then has one less table to worry about." Instead, vox populi should be raised at the highest level of the agenda keepers, because "if pushed, the gate can move with surprising ease."

The gatekeepers' attention can be captured easily. A handful of letters to the editor, and more recently, a couple of faxes, phone calls, or E-mail postings, can quickly focus the minds of media people. It does not necessarily follow that editorial stands will be changed or closely held opinions abandoned. Journalists, the better ones anyway, thrive on lively responses and fresh information: at a minimum, feedback guarantees copy for the next story. We all grow and learn, or try to; but a constantly contorted position of ear-to-the-ground, finger-in-the-air, eye-on-the-weather vane is intellectually ridiculous (as well as awkward). It is bad enough when public officials rely on opinion polls; it would be the end of serious newswork to emulate them.

The public policy gate *does* swing on a ludicrously loose hinge. In 1994, Representative Ron Klink, Democrat from Pittsburgh, introduced House Resolution 4081, a bill proposing that the House and Senate establish an office to do public opinion polling for the U.S. Congress. Ostensibly, Klink took no position on the question of whether the Congress *should* rely so much on polling. Rather, he argued that if the telephone tallies, Perot-style ballots, and other present vox populi forums are all so faulty, then the Congress should hire "scientific" public opinion analysts. That way it would at least have some assurance that the information had some validity. Klink said he was not proposing "government by polling," but added: "there comes a time when leaders need to know the will of the nation on any given subject." Alan Kay, a retired businessman and the founder of the Americans Talk Issues Foundation, supported the Klink bill. Kay fretted that no group is "adequately researching what people want," and so an office of congressional polling would help lawmakers fulfill their "constitutionally assigned responsibility of representing their constituents."[11] A few months later, Newt Gingrich and the House Republican leadership showed that they had been researching "what people want," shaping the language of their Contract with America with the help of Frank Luntz's focus groups.

In the "Federalist Papers," Hamilton, Jay, and Madison also addressed the relationship between representatives and their constituents. These same matters were taken up by the British politician and writer Edmund Burke (1729–1797). In his "Reflections on the Revolution in France," written toward the end of his life, Burke offered what might be considered an early critique of talk-show democracy and its attendant polling madness. "Because half a dozen grasshoppers under a fern make the field ring with their importunate chink," Burke wrote, "whilst thousands of great cattle, reposed underneath the shadow of the British oak, chew the cud and are silent, pray do not imagine that those who make the noise are the only inhabitants of the field . . ." Moreover, in his better-known "Speech to the Electors of Bristol" delivered in November 1774, Burke defended the principle that is undermined by House Resolution 4081, as well as by focus groups and dial groups, Greenberg's and Luntz's, left and right. Burke spoke to the Bristol electorate as a realist who understood what popular democracy required: "It ought to be the happiness and glory of a representative to live in the strictest union, the closest correspondence, and the most unreserved communication with his constituents." But he added: "your representative owes you, not his industry only, but his judgment; and he betrays instead of serving you if he sacrifices it to your opinion."

In the poll-happy, instant call-in culture of the 1990s, a member of Congress who agreed with Burke ran the risk of not getting reelected.

The Hum of the Republic

Among the 1,300 members of President Clinton's White House staff was a group of assistants who arranged presidential telephone conference calls with "opinion leaders," as well as presidential appearances on televised town meetings and radio talk shows. This White House team, headed in the first three years of the Clinton administration by Jeff Eller, a former local-TV producer, went by the formal name Office of Media Affairs. Essentially it was a booking agency, dedicated to placing the bully pulpit of the White House in the service of the president's political agenda. For example, when a key legislative initiative of the president was making its way through the congressional process of committee hearings and preliminary votes, it was the brokers' job to line up talk-show dates, conference calls, and interviews for the president in states where the senators or representatives were still officially undecided or leaning in favor of the proposed law.

Such was the case on a steamy Monday in the summer of 1993, when the Clinton administration's tax package was up for a vote in the House of Representatives. The White House wanted to use Clinton's acknowledged abilities as a mediagenic salesman to advance the bill; the correct spin, or interpretation of the "product" benefits, would be supplied by no less than the president himself. The bookers placed a call to, among others, KNUU radio in Las Vegas, Nevada. They announced the availability of Clinton for a group interview via satellite the next day; was the station interested in the president of the United States (POTUS in White House shorthand)? Within hours, KNUU designated news broadcaster Brenda Pritchard to be one of Clinton's questioners. The next day, Pritchard addressed POTUS via satellite conference call; she asked, rather contentiously, why Clinton expected that the new taxes in his plan could help create jobs. (Later Pritchard told an interviewer that she had made up her mind not to sound "too fluffy.")[1] Almost before KNUU could broadcast its exclusive, the White House had plugged in Clinton for interviews in other key states, a moveable feast of presidential proselytizing, courtesy of satellite uplinks. On Wednesday, the day before the House vote, the bookers lined up journalists in Louisiana for a question-and-answer conference call with the president, and business and political leaders in New Jersey for a presidential conference call. Other conference calls were arranged for journalists and opinionmakers in Arizona and Wisconsin. Paul Schatt, editorial-page editor of the *Arizona Republic* in Phoenix, waited thirty-five minutes on the conference line for his talk with POTUS. The interview reinforced what Schatt had already learned from the Arizona congressional delegation: Clinton was "very smooth, a good politician." Robert Witas, an editorial writer at the *Milwaukee Sentinel,* had the reaction of the been-there-done-that veteran; he had talked to seven presidents in his forty-plus years as a newspaperman. The call did not change his mind, or the *Sentinel's* opposition to the tax plan.

Paul Begala, a presidential adviser and part of the White House war room operation assigned to sell the tax plan, pronounced himself pleased with the direct-appeal effort. Begala acknowledged that the practical effects of the president's calls were "hard to quantify," but he discerned what he called a ripple effect: "even the most jaded person, if he has a conversation with the President of the United States, tends to repeat it."

On the eve of the millennium in America, the reproduction of talk, independent of its content or its effects on the listener, passed for political communications.

The first hands-on presidential spinner was Theodore Roosevelt. White House news conferences began when Roosevelt decided to invite a few reporters into his living quarters for a chat during his morning shave (the description of the White House as a bully pulpit is his). On one level, the satellite conference calls to Pritchard, Schatt et al. represented the natural extension of presidential message from White House to voters' houses. While every president in the last half century has tested available communications modes, past White House staffs often took a perverse pride in working at a *fusty* sort of place. As late as 1992, when George Bush picked up his Oval Office phone, he got a White House operator, not a dial tone. The Clinton administration quickly changed the phone lines and brought in computer workstations, modems, faxes, and E-mail. Ripples of influence emanated from all around Clinton's Washington to the world beyond the beltway. Their effects were, as Begala said, unquantifiable; but the Clintonites were *believers*. Campaign-style war rooms at Justice, the Treasury, and other key cabinet-level departments ran operations intended to shape opinion in favor of specific legislative initiatives (all coordinated, more or less, by the White House). These virtual presidential campaigns reprised the real campaign of 1992. In many cases, they were staffed by the same bright, aggressive, hypereducated, thirtysomething Ivy Leaguers who worked in the 1992 Clinton campaign under George Stephanopoulos, the Ur-bright, aggressive, hypereducated, thirtysomething. The Stephanopoulites, the *New Republic* called them, satirizing a group of lookalike mopheads on its cover. From June 1993 to June 1994, no fewer than 2,000 media interviews were arranged for Clinton and his top administration officials by the bookers.[2]

The Stephanopoulites were like virtuoso children who know how to do one thing well, Macaulay Culkins empowered by their 1992 successes. Having flummoxed the bad-guy opposition once, they were trying to replicate their campaign glory. But sequels, whether in the motion picture business or in political operations, often fail to match the success of the original. The Stephanopoulites found that the channels of the talk-show culture were not easy to manipulate. The White House's use of media put it in heavy, two-way traffic. While the president was reaching out to talk to Pritchard, Schatt, Witas, and other presumed opinionmakers, the hosts of the nation's talk-radio shows were making known their own opinions about Clinton and his administration. In June 1994, *Talkers* magazine, a newsletter serving the National Association of Radio Talk Show Hosts, published its fourth anniversary issue. In the past decade, the number of radio stations using a talk format tripled from 200 to 600, while the association members gained a certain celebrity status. Among the features in the anniversary issue was an interview with Stephanopoulos (a "*Talkers* magazine exclusive") and lists of "The *Talkers*' Ten," the people and topics most frequently discussed on a national cross section of American radio. The list of the ten "Most Criticized Personalities" for the period 1990–1994 was led by Stephanopoulos's boss, Bill Clinton, with Hillary Rodham Clinton next. Number three on the list was the Iraqi dictator Saddam Hussein. The White House might have taken some solace in the knowledge that Dan Quayle and George Bush were numbers four and five on the most criticized list, but only up to a point. The *Talkers*' list was bad news for both Democrats and Republicans; it did not send a very good message about the ideals of representative government either.

Modern communications technologies have placed a bizarre form of political power in the hands of talk-show personalities and call-in hosts. These talkers must fill long stretches of airtime with a signature rhetoric, a distinct style of patter and attitude, or else run the risk of becoming background sound, electronic wallpaper that station managers discard at the drop of a ratings point. In the wired nation, the call-in programs and the talk-show hosts present themselves as facilitators of the "power of the people." In grandiose fashion—the normal mode of much talk discourse—their shows are described as "democracy in action." The existence of new outlets for the exchange of political beliefs and the expression of self-interest *sounds* like a positive, bracing development; it can be taken as evidence that public policy counts. In practice, the talk-show culture too often exchanges only the mutual ignorance of listeners and hosts, who share mainly a taste for ranting and raving. The situation is at once old and familiar, and new and uncharted. Hamilton, Madison, and Jay feared the dangers of factional politics. They saw the need for a central government sufficiently strong to resist the inflamed emotions of the mob. Today, in the blowhard-culture sequel, the "Federalist Papers" would have to defend a constitutional government once again besieged by factions. The writers would find themselves using the old rhetorical terms to deal with a new kind of mob: loudmouths with satellite time. The "Federalist Papers" were comprised of eighty-five letters and ran on for several hundred pages, a lot to ask contemporary audiences to read. The constitutionalists could turn to broadcasting, but Hamilton and friends would need local-station clearances in order to be heard in markets already crowded with talk. Political conversation, as opposed to chatter, might find an audience on PBS, somewhere in the schedule between *Great Performances* and the *Charlie Rose Show*. Al and his co-hosts Jim and Johnny still might come up short, renewal-wise, unless they could adapt their storyline to the needs of entertainment. They would have to develop show-biz schtick and on-air personalities. Above all, the *Feds Show* would have to understand how politics has been steadily reprocessed to make it more useable: another product to feed the twenty-four-hour media machine.

Bill Clinton learned a few lessons about the talk-show culture in his first year in office. Clinton withdrew the name of Zoe Baird, his first nominee for U.S. Attorney General, after the call-in shows made her hiring of an undocumented alien a major "issue" (rather than whatever abilities she might have brought to the job of the nation's chief legal officer). He also backed away from his campaign pledge to end the U.S. military's policy against homosexuals in uniform, after the phone banks of the call-in shows lit up with protests about the end of Western civilization. Again, the Talkers helped inflate a minor and largely symbolic gesture into one more soap-operaish episode in the national entertainment show. There have been homosexuals in the army and navy as long as there has been an army and a navy. But the gays-in-uniform show had to go on: it was good product. Because a blowhard culture makes crude imagery more important than actual ideas, the antigay callers and the administration alike were satisfied when Clinton decided to halt the military's practice of asking new recruits about their sexuality. A nonresolution of a non-event enabled both sides to declare victory.

Well before the talk-show hosts had the Clintons to chew on, the Congress was fodder for a month of drive-time shows. Talk-show hosts helped turn opinion against a 1989 bill to give pay raises to the U.S. Congress. The hosts also were among the loudest advocates for term limits in Congress. (In 1995 the Supreme Court ruled term limits unconstitutional.)[3]

Facts, context, background, balance, ambiguity, the Constitution itself are not allowed to get in the way of talk. The hotter the button, the harder it is pushed. For example, the Home School Legal Defense Association of Purcellville, Virginia, is by any measure a relatively obscure group (it claims 27,000 members). It cared about only one thing: the constitutionally dubious "right of parents" to teach their children at home. The reason why home-schoolers want to do this varies; association members may believe that the public schools promote secular humanism, birth control, godlessness, race-mixing, socialism, feminism, multiculturalism, satanic rites, "un-Christian values," or all of the above. In early 1994 the association leadership misread, either deliberately or sloppily, some fine print in pending federal education legislation and concluded that the "right" to home schooling was somehow in danger. Michael Farris, executive director of the association (and sometime Republican Party candidate for lieutenant governor in Virginia), and six members of his staff appeared by their own count on fifty different radio shows within the span of a few days; all the radio interviews were done, appropriately, by phone at home in Purcellville. The home-schoolers urged listeners to call their congressman to protest the legislation; Farris claimed that 1 million calls flooded Capitol Hill telephone lines, an astonishing, although unprovable figure. But the true number of calls did not matter; the actual wording of the new legislation was not important either. The not-as-described provision was removed anyway, by a vote of 422 to 1. "The grass roots works," Farris claimed.

Grass, or poison ivy? The right to educate one's children at home is just the kind of cause that attracts attention in Talkland. The topic is emotion-laden: the fate of innocent American youth. It polarizes positions, while oversimplifying serious matters. (A worthwhile discussion could be joined, for example, about whether the idea of "America" requires a common civic education, but that would require something more than call-in flaming.) It stirs quasi-paranoidal fears on all sides. Clearly, then, it became good talk product.

Emotional topics are talk-compatible. The Talkers' world is antigovernment, antitax, anti-them. Listeners can fill in their own "them:" secularists, tax-and-spenders, criminals, welfare mothers, blacks and women and gays who seek "special rights," (unlike, say, home-schoolers). The "us" may not necessarily be white, male, and suburban, although those are among the characteristics of both hosts and audience in call-in country. Kenneth Jost in the *Congressional Quarterly Researcher* concluded that the talk shows "have a predominantly conservative orientation." When the Times Mirror Center for the People and the Press surveyed a national sample of 112 talk-show hosts in 1993, it reported that 39 percent said they voted for Clinton, four percentage points less than the 1992 electorate. The survey also found that the call-in shows were more critical of Clinton's programs than the population as a whole. Listener studies by Times Mirror, Simmons Market Research, and other audience surveyors suggest that male callers outnumber female callers by a two to one ratio. Two-thirds of the audience never finished college; the same percentage of listeners earned under $50,000 a year. About 61 percent of the public has listened to talk radio at some time in their lives; one in six listens regularly. One in ten tries to call, but only one in twenty has ever gotten through to ask a question.

Informal experience confirms the largely white-male conservative portrait of hosts and callers. One of our group did two dozen television and radio call-in shows in the course of promoting a recently published book; only one of the hosts encountered was female, and at least nine out of ten callers were males. The only time several women called was during a show with a female host, Diane Rehm of public radio in Washington. The Boston area is typical of metropolitan radio-TV markets. Victoria Jones of WRKO radio was one of two women hosts out of two dozen shows broadcast in the area. Jones was let go in 1994 after one year in Boston. Her employers allowed how it was hard to find talk-show hosts who were both liberal and female and that, over time, she might have built a loyal audience (although the station could not wait). In the weeks before she was fired, Jones took up such topics as the civil war in Bosnia and the case of Lorena Bobbitt (the woman who went on trial for severing her husband's penis). One male caller said Jones should not be talking about Bosnia, because "women can't understand military matters . . ." Another male caller, upset by what he took to be Jones's supportive comments for Lorena Bobbitt, informed Jones that she deserved to be "castrated." Bella English, the columnist for the *Boston Globe* who collected these examples, described one of the usual hometown rants: "So, Jerry, I says to 'em, 'No More Taxes!' I'm sick of all these politicians telling us what to do! I'm moving to New Hampshire!"[4]

On the morning of June 24, 1994, President Bill Clinton decided to descend once again into this overheated talk-show soup.

The ceremonies marking the fiftieth anniversary of D Day were over; the G-7 meetings in Naples lay ahead, and so there was a kind of media lull at the White House during the third week in June 1994. The president was aboard Air Force One on his way to St. Louis. Formally, he was going to inspect a crime-fighting program, but, more practically, he was showing his concern about a subject that, according to the polls, was on the minds of voters all across the country, including those in the battleground state of Missouri. The president's bookers had arranged an interview through satellite phone patch with the A.M. drive-time hosts of KMOX radio, one of the strongest signals in the St. Louis area. The hosts expected a few pleasant moments of the president's time; instead, Clinton answered questions and talked for twenty-three minutes. Caught up himself in the culture of talk radio, he attacked the antagonistic attitudes promoted by talk hosts. The programs "may be fun to listen to, but it's tough to live by." They create "a constant, unremitting drumbeat of negativism and cynicism." Clinton singled out two well-known conservative talkers. One was the television minister, the Reverend Jerry Falwell, who had been selling, via a 1-800 number, a videotape that implied Clinton was implicated in murder and other criminal behavior. The other was Rush Limbaugh, the reigning diva of talk. Limbaugh had "three hours to say whatever he wants . . . and there is no truth detector," the president complained, his voice rising to be heard over the noise of the jet engines.

Falwell and Limbaugh responded the way marketwise entrepreneurs of the 1990s are trained to respond when presented with such an opportunity: they turned the president's criticisms into advertisements for themselves. Falwell announced that his reply would be carried on his syndicated cable program, *The Old Time Gospel Hour* (the same Falwell show that had been flogging the videotape). Later that day, Limbaugh responded by portentously announcing that his anti-Clinton monologues required no verification because "I am the truth detector." The Falwell-Limbaugh bombast was duly recorded the next morning in the *New York Times,* the old-time newspaper of record.

Having lived by the sword of talk, Clinton now pictured himself grievously wounded by that same sword. He should not have been surprised by the rise of the talk-show hosts. Blowhards set the terms of "democratic dialogue" in the years of the Clinton administration and the reign of Speaker Newt Gingrich.

Clinton and Gingrich, Limbaugh and Stern: Noise 'R' Us. America long ago ceased being a manufacturing nation; we are an information-age economy, or so we are told. Men and women now sit at workstations, pushing around text and numbers on computer screens. Leisure has lost its active edge as the fitness craze has waned. But talk continues to expand, like a vast, bloated hot-air balloon: radio talk, TV talk, lawyers' talk, therapists' talk; a gross national product of words, endless, obsessive, and often empty of thought. Talk fills time—drive time, prime time, hangin' out time, whining time, therapy time, retirement time, litigation time. Buffoonish jesters hold court. The political process sputters, which in turn increases the level of the audience's frustration. Party identification is down; voter turnout rates remain among the lowest in the advanced industrial democracies. Whiners call in, threatening "to move to New Hampshire," then hang up and turn up the volume again. We're mad as hell and not taking it anymore . . . just talking about it.

There are growth opportunities in rant-and-rave time. The opéra bouffe Limbaugh is a millionaire; shepherds Falwell, Robertson, and other televangelists have gathered large flocks to shear. Academics and intellectuals, often the last to find out what is going on in the world, have belatedly found their marketing niche, thanks to a company named Planned Television Arts (PTA), which runs a radio interview service that is organized much like the White House bookers' efforts on behalf of POTUS. Authors with a book to promote can sit behind a microphone in PTA's New York studios and reach twenty or more radio shows in a dozen different states within a period of four hours, all without leaving their chairs. Like White House interviews, the PTA service is timed to go West with the sun, starting with East Coast shows and moving across the country to Texas and California. In 1993, for example, author David McCullough sat in New York and "traveled" to a dozen cities, doing interviews with talk-show hosts to promote the paperback edition of his book on Harry Truman. Author McCullough was amazed at the ceaseless talk, from early morning to late at night: "the hum of the Republic," he called it. During McCullough's day at PTA, he informed his phone mate at WTIC radio in Hartford, Connecticut, that "we live in a world where nothing is as it seems; all is contrivance." There was no sign that he was being ironic.

In its cover story for March 14, 1994, *Business Week* magazine trumpeted the rise of America's "entertainment economy." The magazine used Bureau of Labor Statistics data to calculate that the U.S. entertainment and recreation industries added 200,000 workers in 1993, "a stunning 12 per cent of all net new employment." Further, in 1992 Americans spent $430 billion "on old fashioned and new fangled ways to amuse themselves," from video rentals to gambling. America's growth engines, *Business Week* concluded, were its theme parks, casinos, sports—and interactive TV.

American politics and the processes of governing, in their contemporary forms at least, are well positioned to participate in the emerging entertainment economy. Presidential campaigning has long been treated as a sport; high among the indictments of political journalists is the charge that they pay too much attention to "horse race coverage." As for government, Washington has become a kind of theme park. Electronic town meetings, the talk shows, the call-ins, and the other interactive forms have demonstrated their amusement value. When the Odyssey company, a market research firm based in Silicon Valley, held focus groups in 1993 and 1994 to probe attitudes about the new technologies, it found that most people were not interested in any of the promised interactive *information* services. According to Nicholas Donatiello, president and chief executive officer of Odyssey, consumers really desired better at-home entertainment. Before helping to start Odyssey, Donatiello worked on Capitol Hill for Senator Daniel Patrick Moynihan.[5]

The White House's vision of its high-technology future remained undimmed. The president was not yet computer literate, for all of his Rhodes Scholar's intelligence. But Vice President Gore filled the role of hacker-in-chief in the Clinton administration. In January 1994, he participated in an online conference, a computer-to-computer version of an electronic town meeting. The editors of *U.S. News & World Report* sponsored the forum to publicize the availability of the magazine's contents on the CompuServe network. At the announced time, Gore, a CompuServe moderator, and interested CompuServe subscribers came together in cyberspace; an audience scattered around the country put questions to the moderator via computer and the moderator relayed them to Gore in Washington. There were some disquieting parallels in the online conference to talk television and radio. Some 900 people "showed up" (by trying to log on); around 300 got through to the moderator's screen and, in the time allotted, only 10 were able to put a question to Gore. The sponsors estimated that about the same number are heard in a typical hourlong talk show on radio.[6]

In the spring of 1995, the consulting firm Jupiter Communications estimated that over 6 million Americans belonged to one or another of the large commercial computer-communications services like CompuServe, Prodigy, America Online, and Delphi. Overall, perhaps 30 million computer owners worldwide were using the Internet, the putative working prototype of the information superhighway. In anticipation of the day when as many Americans as own a radio or television will have the computer-modem ability to go online, the White House Office of Communications sought the help of the Artificial Intelligence (AI) Laboratory at MIT. The AI Lab, under a pro bono contract, began developing a software program to analyze the contents of computer messages coming into the White House and to forward them to the appropriate office or agency. Onliners who send a message to the White House would be asked to follow a standard electronic form (name, address, organization, information being requested, approximate category for registering opinion, etc.). The suitably formatted text would then be analyzed by a computer programmed to look for key words. A citizen's message with, say, the words "intervention" and "Haiti" would go to the State Department; "medicare" and "costs" could generate the text of a health-care speech by Hillary Rodham Clinton in response. Eventually, more advanced software could use "natural-language-recognition techniques" to tease out the tone of each message—anger, approval, whatever. By the millennium, White House computers could be programmed to produce a cumulative attitudinal analysis of all the messages received. The twenty-first century president would have available a daily poll of the online electorate.[7]

The Clinton staffer working with the AI Lab was Jock Gill, the same techie who put the White House online in early 1993 (chapter 4). Gill was given the title of "Director of Public Access, E-mail and Electronic Publishing, White House Office of Communications," a newly created position. Gill has described his work as "connecting the government and the people." More accurately, computers rather than humans will be linked: virtual democracy, not flesh-and-blood democracy. Perhaps that is the best we can expect in a society as sprawling, unruly, and harried as ours.

Computer democracy spreads political communications farther and faster than ever before, but not deeper. At the end of 1994, the White House launched its World Wide Web site on the Internet; users were connected to a virtual White House and quickly explored what became a main attraction: a digitized photographic tour of the president's house (the virtual visitors even signed a "guest book" to record their trip). The promise of access was fulfilled, but with little relationship to democratic governance.

The White House browsers at least benefited from a light history lesson. It would be hard to pinpoint what advantages other users are deriving from the new media. The best that can be said about talk radio may be that it provides an outlet for venting some of the anger endemic in America. Toxic as much of this talk is, it can sound like the *MacNeil/Lehrer NewsHour* compared to some of the discourse on E-mail and various online chat groups. Radio hosts have to pay lip service to minimal good taste and the laws against libel.

Critics who scoff at high-technology efforts to aid political communications between governors and governed too often sound like Luddites, Gutenberg-age reactionaries intent on throwing a wrench into the cybergears. But technology is just that: dumb machinery that requires the animating spirit of human intelligence. The ultimate purpose of this narrative is not to argue against new communications modes, but to plea for the primacy of content in those communications. In the past, times of great social crisis in America fortuitously have produced great leaders capable of mobilizing public resolve. The authors of the "Federalist Papers" moved a divided audience with cogently written briefs. Later, during civil war, depression, global conflicts, and unsettled peace, plain-speaking presidents rallied hesitant citizens with the power of the spoken word. If Online America is to find its own Madisons or Roosevelts or Trumans, it will have to attend to the software, as always.

The Newtonian Devolution

The day was mild, the sun bright for late September. Marshals passed out small, starchy American flags. Then, 150 Republican members of the U.S. House of Representatives and some 200 GOP challengers, who hoped to become incumbents when the 104th Congress convened in January 1995, marched five abreast to the west front of the Capitol. The group took assigned positions on the broad stone steps, standing before a twenty-foot-high map of the United States with the words "Contract With America" printed in white letters. The scene was composed as exquisitely as a Japanese floral arrangement: one black face to stage left in the sea of blue-suited, rep-tied men; two women, also in dressed-for-success suits, just to the right of stage center. The cameras rolled. There were prayers, the Pledge of Allegiance. The band played "This is My Country"—an amazingly accurate prediction, it turned out.

Six weeks later, when the votes were counted on election night 1994, not one of the Republican incumbents lost; stunningly, no fewer than seventy-three of those challengers who had gathered on the Capitol steps were elected. In the Senate, the story was the same. For the first time in forty years, the Republicans controlled both houses of Congress. Bill Clinton's presidency had been judged DOA within a week of his inauguration by the glib Sunday talk-show morticians; After the November vote, it was pronounced dead again, this time with a stake driven through its heart and salt scattered around the burial ground.

The Republican Revolution, commentators called it. Actually, it was more a restoration, a return to old themes presented in traditional media formats. The "Contract With America" symbolically nationalized the election, presenting a single powerful image for the network news show and morning papers. But it was already a contest that the Republicans could not lose. For three decades, the country had been moving to the right, a move masked by the disgrace of the venomous Nixon (which helped elect Jimmy Carter) and the bumbling of the Bush years (the proximate cause of Clinton's election). But while the presidency all but belonged to the Republicans in the last third of the century, the remnants of the New Deal coalition helped keep the Democrats in control of the Congress. By 1994, the congressional Democrats were moribund, too. The South was solid again . . . for conservatives. In the North, the children of ethnic blue-collar workers now lived in the suburbs, belonged to a new class of computer-technology-office workers, and voted Republican. The Clinton administration had allowed itself to become identified with homosexual rights and gun control—"gays and guns," in Hillary Rodham Clinton's blunt summing-up (if she had been completely candid, she would have added, ". . . and gangs of blacks"). A poll on the eve of the November 1994 election by the Times-Mirror Center for the People and the Press showed that the three demographic groups most motivated to vote against President Clinton were Southern white males, evangelical Christians, and regular talk-radio listeners.

The conventional wisdom also misread the Republicans' "Contract With America." The mainstream press rightly judged the ten-point contract to be a poll-driven document, the result of focus groups and interest-centered surveys. The Contract, skeptics pointed out, contained simple solutions presented in the sound-bite style of the talk-show culture. But these "defects"—from the point of view of "serious" discourse—made the Contract irresistible to target audiences. It was a Christmas wish list for the good families of the middle class, with something special for each Republican constituency: balanced budget, crime busting, line-item veto, cuts in the capital gains tax and in government regulations, welfare reform, more dollars for the military, tax credits for families with children, even for those making $200,000 a year—all packaged with the beribboned promise that the new majority would bring up for vote each of the ten points within the first 100 days of the 104th Congress.

Only belatedly did the commentators recognize that the "Contract With America" was a shrewd combination of hot-button words and potent patriotic imagery. Finally, too, the mainstream press began paying closer attention to the man behind the marketing, Newt Gingrich, the congressman from Cobb County outside Atlanta and the new Speaker of the House. With the election of the Republican majority, Gingrich became an instant celebrity. The *New York Times* alone devoted two dozen separate editorials and op-ed pieces to Gingrich in the period from November 10 to December 10—and this coverage did not include Gingrich stories in the *Times'* news pages. Gingrich had been in Washington since 1979; he was hardly an enigmatic figure.

The public Gingrich presented himself as an enemy of the dominant liberal media. In fact, the real Gingrich had spent the past fifteen years learning to master the publicity techniques of the media establishment. He instructed junior colleagues, for example, on the importance of getting to know television news directors and their needs. Gingrich assiduously worked both sides of the street, presenting camera-ready events for the mainstream media, while exploiting the possibilities of cable and satellite television. He had his own weekly call-in show, *Progress Report,* which was cablecast live on Tuesdays at 10 P.M. eastern time on the conservative cable system, National Empowerment Television. Beginning in 1993, Gingrich also presided over "Renewing American Civilization," a twenty-hour distance-learning course, offered via satellite to college classrooms under the nominal auspices of Reinhardt College in Waleska, Georgia. The actual sponsor was the Progress and Freedom Foundation, run by Gingrich confidant Jeffrey Eisenach, and itself funded by contributions from drug companies and other firms with a direct stake in the outcome of congressional legislation. The foundation also underwrote Gingrich's call-in show on NET. Among the foundation's other activities, it has studied ways to speed up the licensing and testing of new medical technologies, "a matter of intense interest to the health industry," the *New York Times* drily reported. Shortly after the November elections, the foundation distributed a "Magna Carta for the Knowledge Age," calling for the deregulation of every aspect of telecommunications—more sweet sounds for industry, this time for the cable, wireless communications, and computer businesses.

As much as anybody in the Washington media-political complex he so reviled, Gingrich moved familiarly along those same avenues of influence. He presented his cable show activities as something of a public service. Because the "elite media" so often distort events he said on his show on December 6, the call-ins on *Progress Report* mean that "the people can have a dialogue." But Gingrich's ambitions go far beyond the viewers of a cable system reaching less than 5 percent of the national television audience. Perhaps 1996 is too soon for Gingrich to turn his back on the Speaker's post and run all-out for the Republican presidential nomination; then again, he will be just 56 the next time around, in 2000.

The rise of Newt Gingrich presents an eerie parallel. In 1992, Bill Clinton came to power in part by calling himself a "New Democrat," stressing the single theme of "change," and mounting the underutilized bully pulpits of the talk shows, TV town meetings, and drive-time radio. Clinton also was helped by the candidacy of Ross Perot. Another self-proclaimed populist of new media, Perot took enough votes away from Bush to help elect Clinton. Gingrich is the 1995 model of 1992 Clinton-Perot, tooling along with a simple high concept: the liberal welfare state has failed, and must be destroyed. Gingrich also resuscitated Ronald Reagan's 1980s conservatism, cleverly integrating the standard complement of strong emotive words—"freedom," "enterprise," "strength," "family"—with the new-media technologies and with talk of the free-market wonders of telecommunications. He was a smarter, faster-talking, younger Reagan. And a meaner Reagan, as well: The Gipper merely shook his old, dyed head at "welfare queens" (code word for "shiftless black women"). Gingrich proposed to put their children in orphanages, a return to the *1880s*.

Gingrich became a tempting target for the hounds of the press, just as Clinton had been earlier. Gingrich's backward-looking proposals for a kind of nineteenth-century unfettered capitalism, complete with alms houses, were accompanied by a technocrat's futuristic vision. After his Republican colleagues named him Speaker by acclamation, Gingrich described how, in the millennium, "every American will have a cellular phone," to link him to the global marketplace. Moreover, electorate and representatives alike would be interconnected by computer, fax, and modem. The Gingrichian vision of cybernetic democracy elicited some liberal titters. "Lost in space," the *New Yorker* said, by way of summing up Gingrich's airy talk of lunar bases, "religious software," and "demassified civilization." When Gingrich attacked the "McGovernik counter-culture" and suggested that Bill and Hillary Clinton and their White House staff were not "normal" Americans, the magazine said, he himself came across as obsessive, even "weird."

Newt Gingrich was easier to mock than to understand. His rise, along with the GOP victory of 1994, completes the narrative. The talk-show culture has produced a tale full of sound bites and suburban fury. In early December 1994, the incoming class of Republican representatives—the same hopefuls who had assembled on the Capitol steps in September—presented a lapel pin to Rush Limbaugh. The pin read: "Majority Maker." At the same meeting, former Congressman Vin Weber, an official of the conservative group, Empower America, actually used the phrase "the Limbaugh Congress." (According to the GOP pollster Frank Luntz, people who listened to ten hours or more of talk radio a week voted Republican in 1994 by a three-to-one margin—figures confirming the Times Mirror survey.) Limbaugh himself correctly concluded that his radio and TV shows had merely "validated" the feelings of the electorate, which has been "conservative in its heart for the longest time."

The Republicans wrested power from the Democrats in 1994, then, with a traditional message promoted through tested media techniques. In the end, it was special-interest politics, smartly retrofitted for the new media landscape. The "Rush Majority" had determined what the likeliest voters wanted, as expressed in polls and call-in shows, and delivered it to them.

Fair enough. That is how the political process now works in Virtual America. Those who don't like the results are free to fashion their own political strategies, using the full panoply of media—old, new, hyper—to deliver their messages. In the end, no democrat (with a small d) can be against talk, even the talk of the blowhards. As Justice Brandeis suggested, the answer to bad speech is not censorship or silence, but more speech. The key to genuine communication through any medium, in any century, is that someone must take the time to listen, and to think.

Acknowledgments

Most of the reporting and research for this book was done when we were colleagues in the department of journalism at New York University. We thank NYU and especially Dean C. Duncan Rice and Professor Mitchell Stephens for their support and encouragement. We also thank the Annenberg Washington Program in Communications Policy Studies. This work could not have been completed without the support of Annenberg Washington Program director Newton N. Minow and executive director Yvonne Zecca. We are especially grateful to Stephen Bates, Annenberg senior fellow (and longtime friend), for contributing both shrewd advice and key archival data. The staff at The MIT Press has been exemplary; we thank in particular Terry Vaughn, Ann Sochi, and Melissa Vaughn. A number of others aided our research and understanding. We wish to mention Nina Biddle, Richard Frank, Gregg Geller, Kate Gerwig, Ruth Gurevitch, Ellen Hume, David Klein, Edward Kosner, Wendy Martens, Chuck Martin, Martha McKay, Eric Moskal, Kara Newman, Sara Olkon, Gregory Payne, Lori Robinson, John Simerman, Richard David Story, John Fox Sullivan, David White, and Lora Zaretsky. Portions of this book appeared in different form in the *American Behavioral Scientist, National Journal, New York* magazine, and *TV Guide.* Chapter sources and notes appear on the pages that follow. All conclusions and opinions are our own.

Notes

Introduction

1. For a good discussion of these developments, see William Schneider, "Coarsening of Public Life Continues," *National Journal*, May 21, 1994. Schneider examined the Clarence Thomas-Anita Hill spectacle and the charges brought by Paula Jones against Bill Clinton.

Chapter 1

1. Stephen Hess, the Brookings Institution scholar, calculated that almost half of the 5 percent increase in turnout in the presidential elections from 1988 to 1992 may have been due to "the new ways" the candidates used to reach voters. See Hess, "President Clinton and the White House Press Corps—Year One," *Media Studies Journal*, spring 1994. The journal is a publication of the Freedom Forum Media Studies Center.

2. Reporter Jennifer Allen visited the control room of KTVU, Oakland to provide a hilarious account of Brown's "call-in karma." See "Radio Daze," *New Republic*, May 2, 1994.

3. Jeff Greenfield, the ABC News analyst, was among the first to comment on this change in the Clinton style.

Chapter 2

1. For a good account of FDR and his fireside manner, see Arthur Schlesinger, Jr., *The Age of Roosevelt: The Coming of the New Deal* (Boston: Houghton Mifflin, 1957).

2. For a further account and analysis of the Father Coughlin phenomenon, see Alan Brinkley's *Voices of Protest* (New York: Vintage, 1983).

3. Our colleague Stephen Bates viewed much of the film materials at the National Archives in Washington. The narrative here draws heavily from his observations.

4. In the 1970s and 1980s, Garth ran the media campaigns for candidate and then-Mayor Edward I. Koch of New York. In 1992, Garth worked for Republican Senator Arlen Specter in Pennsylvania; two years later, he was working for Mario Cuomo, the Democratic governor of New York.

5. Squier went on to produce candidate Jimmy Carter's 1976 election-eve show, and in 1992 he was a senior wise man for the Clinton-Gore media campaign. He continued as an adviser to the Clinton White House through the mid-1990s, while regularly appearing as a Democratic Party commentator on the NBC *Today* show.

6. Other examples of Guggenheim's work for McGovern, as well as almost 2,000 hours of political-advertising materials, are now preserved on video in the archives of the News Study Group, Department of Journalism, New York University.

Chapter 3

1. Timothy Crouse, *The Boys on the Bus* (New York: Random House, 1973), p. 223.

2. Martha McKay and Wendy Martens, our former associates at the News Study Group, conducted most of the interviews with the women and men covering the 1992 campaign.

3. Edwin Diamond, Gregg Geller, and Heidi Ruiz, "Watching the Hillary Watchers . . ." *National Journal* April 24, 1993.

4. Ted Koppel, the host of ABC's *Nightline,* was a television correspondent in Vietnam in the late 1960s. In a speech at Harvard in the spring of 1994, he contrasted the "more leisurely" pace of TV journalism then with the contemporary style of fire-ready-aim. Then, "you [had] some time to think." Today, with portable-TV ground stations and satellite phones, reporters can be on the air live from anywhere in the world at any time, no matter how prepared or unprepared they may be. "The technological tail is wagging the editorial dog," Koppel said.

5. The Freedom Forum report was made available to us by staff member Dirk Smilie.

6. See Tom Rosenstiel, "The New High-Tech Press Pack," *Media Critic,* spring 1994.

7. Other designations of the eighteen to twenty-eight year-old group were less generous: slackers, generation X, twentynothings.

8. For a good account of the MTV culture and the youth market, see Jonathan S. Cohn, "MTV: Programming Intended Less To Offend Than To Sell," *The National Times,* April/May 1994. Cohn claims that MTV began covering the 1992 campaign after "market data indicated that the audience craved politics—specifically left-leaning politics."

Chapter 4

1. Both the *American Spectator* and the *Los Angeles Times* stories were more fully analyzed in Edwin Diamond, "Gennifer, Part Two," *New York* magazine, January 17, 1994.

2. Data compiled by Sharon Warden, "Clinton Loses Support Over Foreign Policy," *Washington Post,* May 17, 1994. See also "Whitewater Weighs Down Clinton in Public's Eyes," one of the occasional papers of the Times Mirror Center for the People and the Press, March 25, 1994. The plunge in the president's public approval ratings prompted one commentator to write about "the brittleness" of the Clinton presidency. See George Will, "The Porcelain Presidency," *Newsweek,* July 25, 1994.

3. Keen was among the first to write about the health-care marketing plan. See also Dana Priest, "Flawed Sales Pitch Blamed For Health Reform Setbacks," *Washington Post,* March 30, 1994.

4. The interviews and analyses were done by our News Study Group at New York University. See Edwin Diamond, Ruth Gurevitch, and Robert Silverman, "Using the Old And New Media to Sell Clinton's Programs to the Public," *National Journal,* November 21, 1993.

5. These findings are based on a sample of 372 magazine and newspaper articles collected by Gregg Geller of the News Study Group. Representative tapes of network television news coverage were also examined.

6. See Clarence Page, "Help for the Confused Political Wife," *Chicago Tribune,* March 22, 1992.

Chapter 5

1. The ABC News program *Nightline* found a broadcast interview from 1970 in which Perot talked about using technology to create electronic town meetings and organize a new party.

2. Garry Wills, "Perot Will Undo Himself Again, But Until Then . . ." *Dallas Morning News,* June 6, 1993. See also Laurence Barrett, "Heckler in Chief," *Time* magazine, March 29, 1993.

3. The phrase "national conversation" sounds like a contradiction in terms; worse, to urge more talk in logorrheic America seems akin to suggesting that midtown New York City needs more automobile traffic. Chairman Hackney offered a defense of the idea in "Organizing a National Conversation," *The Chronicle of Higher Education,* April 20, 1994. He also appeared in a C-SPAN interview show to promote his proposal, taking listeners' calls from around the country. Before coming to NEH, Hackney was a university president and a historian by training whose first books explored . . . American populism.

4. To find out how much "democracy" actually existed in Perot's own organization, a member of our group sent in the required annual dues to United We Stand America and received a "founding member" card. The accompanying letter promised that "organizing at every level in the country" will begin "in the next few weeks." The letter added: "You will be contacted." The letter was dated March 8, 1993. The only "contact" over the next eighteen months were computer-generated mailings asking for more donations.

5. Edwin Diamond, Gregg Geller, and John Simerman, "Press Creates a Role for Perot," *National Journal,* December 11, 1993.

6. For a good examination of Perot's "understanding" of international trade policy, see James Bovard, "Sucking Sound," *New Republic,* September 20–27, 1993.

7. *Newsday* obtained a copy of the checklist. See David Firestone, "Don't Forget the Chocolate," *Newsday,* May 9, 1993.

8. General Donald Dawson was an aide to Truman in this period; he recalled the MacArthur meetings at a panel discussion held in Chicago to mark the fiftieth anniversary of Truman's nomination to the vice presidency. "I Remember Truman: A Symposium," Chicago Cultural Center, July 21, 1994.

Chapter 6

1. The Sega channel is a virtual channel, because it takes up no space on cable bandwidth. It embeds its data stream onto cable transmissions from head-end to user. The channel can be accessed only by users owning Sega Genesis machines and special converters. The Sega channel was more fully analyzed in Robert Silverman, "Sega Channels TV Vidgames," *Variety*, July 18–24, 1994.

2. In June, 1994, the plan for a music-and-shopping network that would rival MTV was shelved when one of the principals became involved in merger talks with the parent company of MTV. But the idea was too good to let die: the slacker generation usually finds energy enough to shop. So do their parents. No fewer than six new shopping channels have been proposed. And for the grandparents, the Health channel designed to sell vitamins and prescription drugs, is awaiting FDA approval.

3. The FCC's retransmission rules explained why Turner Classic Movies, from Turner Broadcasting; fX, from the Fox network; and America's Talking, from NBC, were able to gain access to cable systems relatively easily. The cable operators agreed with Turner, Fox, and NBC to carry their new channels in return for receiving the "free carriage" of, respectively, the Turner, Fox, and NBC network schedules. The FCC rules were intended to make such a deal possible. What government taketh, it also giveth.

4. Mitchell Stephens, *A History of News* (New York: Viking, 1988).

5. Diana McClellan makes a point that the *Post* skittishly avoided. She believed her report to be true and says that she still "stands by" the story. Private communication, April 30, 1993.

Chapter 7

1. The Hessert interview and the other materials on the handlers grew out of a News Study Group project. NSG members Nina Biddle, Wendy Martens, and Martha McKay did the majority of the reporting.

2. In 1993, "War Room" was nominated by the motion picture academy in Hollywood for an Oscar in the documentary category—a wonderful conflation of entertainment and politics. The film did not win.

3. *The New Republic,* July 19–26, 1993.

4. Stern ended his "run" for office after he learned that New York law required candidates to disclose their incomes.

5. *Newsweek* was among the first mainstream publications to write in-depth about the talk-show culture. The magazine pointed out that conservatives have used broadcasting to reach their audiences long before Limbaugh and the current group of talk-show hosts opened their mouths. In the 1930s, William Pelley and Gerald L. K. Smith, as well as the radio priest Father Charles Coughlin, were counterpoints to Roosevelt; later, in the postwar years, Paul Harvey had more outlets than any other commentator. In the 1980s, Boston talk host Jerry Williams regularly railed against then-Governor Michael Dukakis and the cost of big government in "Tax-achusetts." Williams also helped bring about the repeal of the Massachusetts seatbelt law (this simple safety measure was regarded as a symbol of the "intrusive" state). See Howard Fineman, "The Power of Talk," *Newsweek,* February 8, 1993.

6. The talk-show guy culture continues to spread. In the summer of 1994, songs and skits on Don Imus's *Imus in the Morning* dealt with Hillary Rodham Clinton's menstruation and with gay Native Americans, called, naturally, Navahomos. In the Clinton years, Imus began being heard in Washington, and Bill Bradley, the U.S. senator from New Jersey, became a regular interviewee.

7. The liberal media-watchdog group Fairness and Accuracy in Reporting (FAIR) compiled a list of over a dozen Limbaugh misstatements and fabrications, which they published in their "Extra" newsletter in the summer of 1994.

Chapter 8

1. The pay was $200 for a one-hour session; the money was handed over at the end, mafioso-style, in a plain brown envelope containing two crisp, new, $100 bills.

2. See James Barnes "The Persona Plays in Peoria . . .", *National Journal,* Feb. 20, 1993, p. 474.

3. Among the early students of "demographic politics" were the late MIT political scientist Ithiel de Sola Pool and his associate Samuel Popkin. Pool's book, *The Technologies of Freedom,* was optimistic about the new communications modes. It correctly foresaw the decline of totalitarian regimes in the world of new media. The book was published in 1983, seven years before the fall of the Soviet state.

4. James Perry, "Clinton Relies Heavily on White House Pollster to Take Words Right Out of the Public's Mouth," *Wall Street Journal,* March 23, 1994. For the purposes of this book, one of our group used the words "convenience" and "control" to describe what was desired in personal communications in the

AT & T interview mentioned in this chapter. We are watching to see if these markers show up in a product-promotion campaign.

5. James Barnes, "Polls Apart," *National Journal,* July 10, 1993.

6. The results of the referendum are contained in a letter dated April, 26, 1993 that was sent out to United We Stand America members over the signature of Ross Perot.

7. John Leo, "The Junking of History," *U.S. News & World Report,* February 28, 1994.

8. David Broder cited these figures in "War on Cynicism," *Washington Post,* July 6, 1994.

9. Such uses of 1-900 numbers are known as SLOPS, for self-selected, listener-oriented public survey. See Sheldon Gawiser, president of the National Council on Public Polls, quoted by Frazier Moore, Associated Press national wire, June 27, 1994.

10. The booklet sold for $4.95 postpaid; it included addresses of major media outlets. See also Reed Irvine, "AIM Report," November 1993.

11. See Adam Clymer, "Proposal in Congress to Erase Polling Gap," *New York Times,* May 15, 1994.

Chapter 9

1. Pritchard was interviewed by Mike Feinsilber of the Associated Press. See "White House Calling," Associated Press national wire, August 5, 1993.

2. The figure was reported by Andrea Mitchell of NBC News.

3. See the excellent report by Kenneth Jost, *CQ Researcher,* a publication of the *Congressional Quarterly,* spring 1994.

4. English offered to pay the caller's car tolls if he would take "100 of his buddies with him, and thereby raise Massachusetts' collective IQ by several points."

5. Donatiello described his findings at a seminar convened in Washington, D.C., by Ellen Hume at the offices of the Annenberg Washington Program, May 18, 1994.

6. For an account of Gore's conference, see Mary Kathleen Flynn, "Talk Shows in Cyberspace," *U.S. News & World Report,* July 14, 1994. In March 1994, in the course of promoting a new book, one of our group participated in the regular 9 P.M. EST America Online forum, "Center Stage Interview,"

answering questions about the book's findings. The writer sat by his phone in New York City and the interviewers sent their questions via computer to a "master of ceremonies" in suburban Washington, who selected the ones to relay. By and large, the questions were good. Several reflected a knowledge of the subject. America Online, April 14, 1994.

7. The AI-White House project was described in the MIT magazine *Technology Review,* July 1993.

Index
